Just Thinking

By

Cathy Brown

ISBN 978-0-578-13723-0

Just Thinking: A Time to Marvel

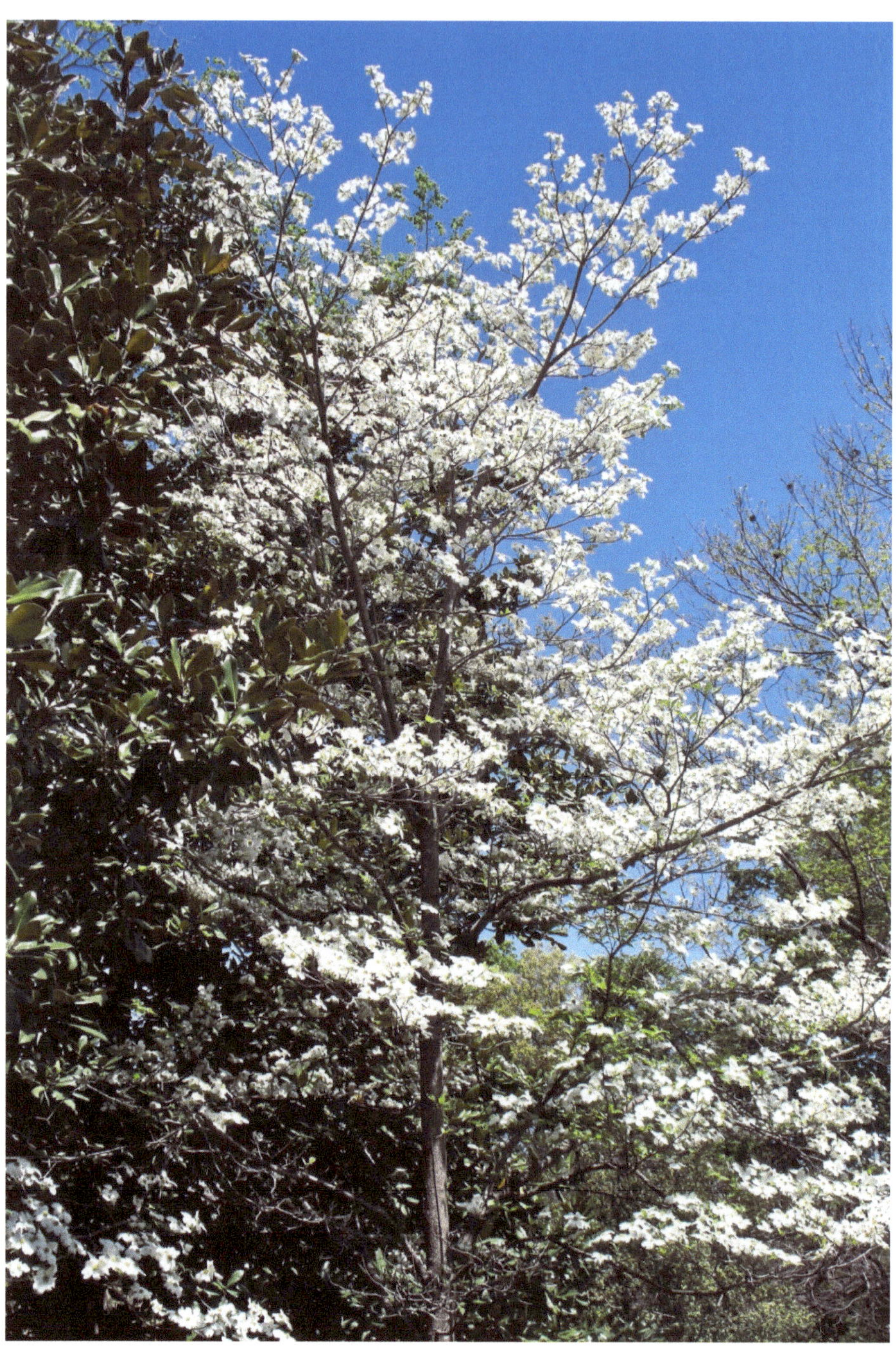

Dogwood Trees in the Spring Time

The Jewels of Nature Edition: Preface

People enter the world as innocent human beings at birth with no awareness of how or why we were created. All we know is that the gift of life was presented to us for an undetermined period of time. Along with that gift, we are also given the ability to choose how we want to use it. Naturally, people want to make the most of this amazing treasure. So, the logical next step is to explore the reasons we were created; with that basic knowledge, we have a stepping stone that can lead us to find the purpose of our individual lives. Medical science seems to suggest that having a purpose tends to enhance our physical health, as well. This basic human drive to find the answers to our origin and purpose is what is called "spirituality".

If my spirituality is so important to the quality of my life, how do I go about addressing it?

Spirituality must be nurtured. It starts with peace and TRANQUILITY. When we allow time in our busy lives to slow down, it is much easier to find serenity. There are numerous ways to slow ourselves down long enough to nurture our spirituality. Some of my favorites are:

- Arising an hour early in the mornings in order to gracefully slide into the day
- Practicing living in the moment, rather than thinking about the future or the past
- Fly fishing on a tranquil alpine lake
- Hiking down a pristine mountainside in the snow
- Turning off the television or telephone
- Sipping iced tea on a summer day while lounging in a gazebo
- Waking up to the sound of birds chirping in the morning

Once a tone of tranquility is set, the next step is to MARVEL. Take the time to look around you. Notice what is beautiful or inspiring or amazing. Make the effort to experience all of your sensations-sight, hearing, smell, touch, and taste. Let them soak into your psyche.

Lastly, it is time to EXPLORE. A good way to do this is by reading the works of philosophers and other wise authors. Embrace what rings true in your own experience and what makes sense in your own mind. And don't forget to enjoy the process of the quest for truth!

REFLECTION is the combination of these three concepts---nurturing tranquility, marveling over the mysteries in life, and exploring in the search for truth. Take time, on a frequent and regular basis, for quiet reflection. It gives us a chance to gain the insights that are so crucial for a richer, fuller life! That is what this book is all about!

Just Thinking: From the Author

Dear Readers,

This book is meant to share my own spiritual adventure with you. It is designed to be a 21-day trek into exciting and possibly unfamiliar territory. Experts say it takes that amount of time to develop a habit; my goal is to help you start a daily routine with the intent to reflect upon your origin and life purpose. It can give you a good start toward nurturing your own spirituality.

We will use several concepts to do that. They are as follows:

- Displaying images to marvel about
- Choosing a topic to explore
- Sharing personal stories
- Depicting positive living skills

One of the purposes of this endeavor is to demonstrate a way to enhance your quest for a healthier spiritual life. Steps used to accomplish this are:

- Setting a therapeutic atmosphere
- Marveling about beautiful, inspiring, amazing things
- Exploring a variety of topics that can enhance the quality of life

Exploration is a vital part of nurturing your spirituality. There is an unfathomable amount of literature on this topic, but, in this book, I have chosen to explore what the Bible has to say about life. I invite you to join me on this adventure!

In this volume, you will learn more about me as we go along. By the end of our three weeks together, you will find that I am a great lover of the outdoors; but it may be surprising to learn that, it was only in my mid-fifties, that I came to appreciate it. However, once my husband took me on the first camping trip, I was "hooked". I grew up as a studious "book-worm" with absolutely no interest in or aptitude for anything physically challenging. I did not even like to be out in the sun. My interests/hobbies have been creative writing and photography. But, in the last few years, I have learned to love hiking, biking, kayaking, fly fishing, snow shoeing, snowmobiling, and even white water rafting. Now, I am not saying that I am especially adept at any of these sports, but I am SO thankful to have learned to embrace them early enough to make these activities a part of my life for a long time to come. As you explore the pages in this volume, I hope you will enjoy my amateur photography, knowing that virtually every photo is from my personal excursions. Another thing you should know is that, for the purposes of this book, I claim no professional authority on any topic whatsoever. I am simply sharing what I think. Resolve to explore for yourself so that you can find your own truth, because borrowing someone else's beliefs cannot be very satisfying. On that note, it is time to start our spiritual adventure in Just Thinking!

Sincerely,
Cathy Foster Brown

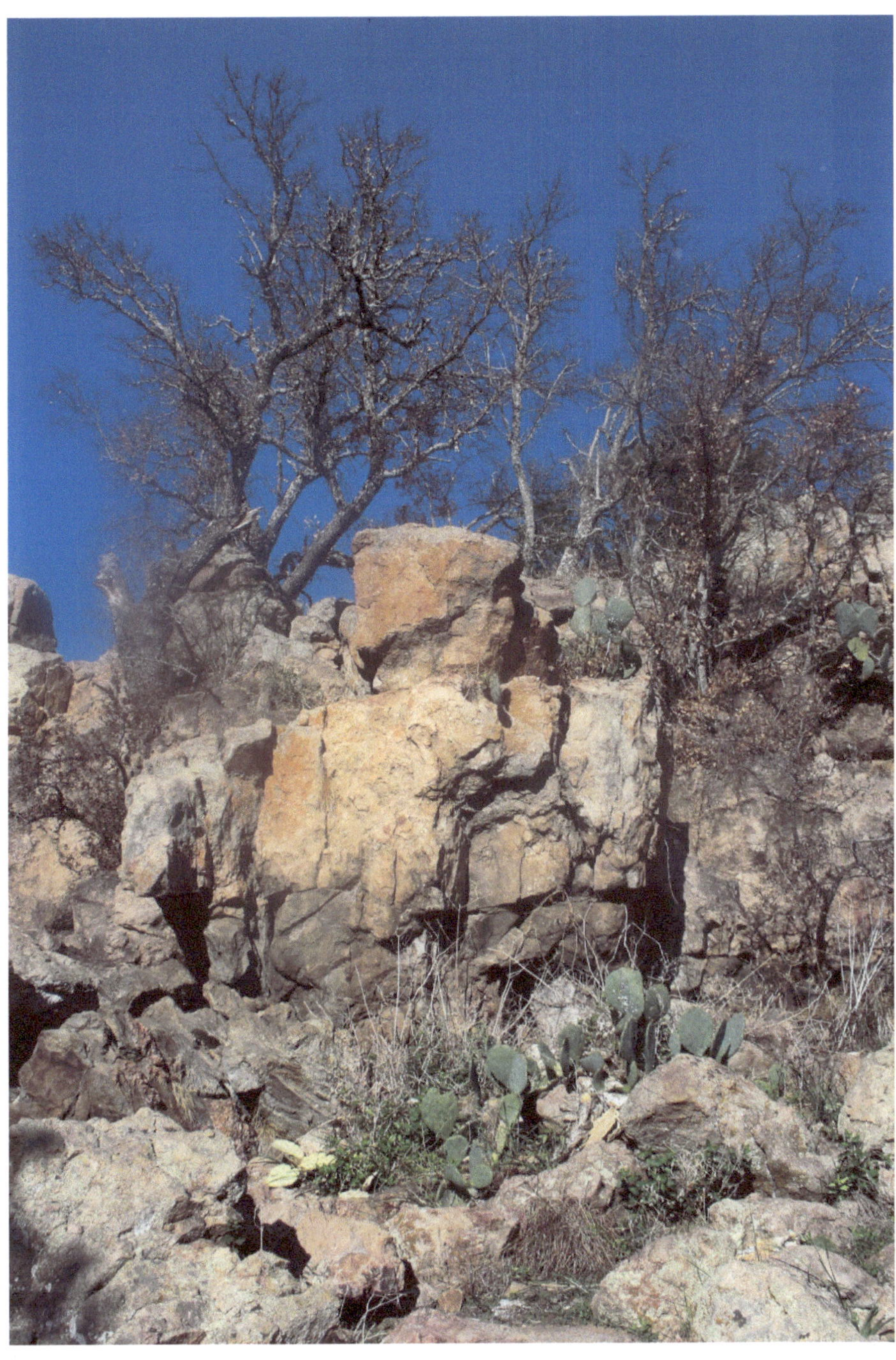

Camping Amidst Rugged Beauty

Just Thinking: A Time to Marvel

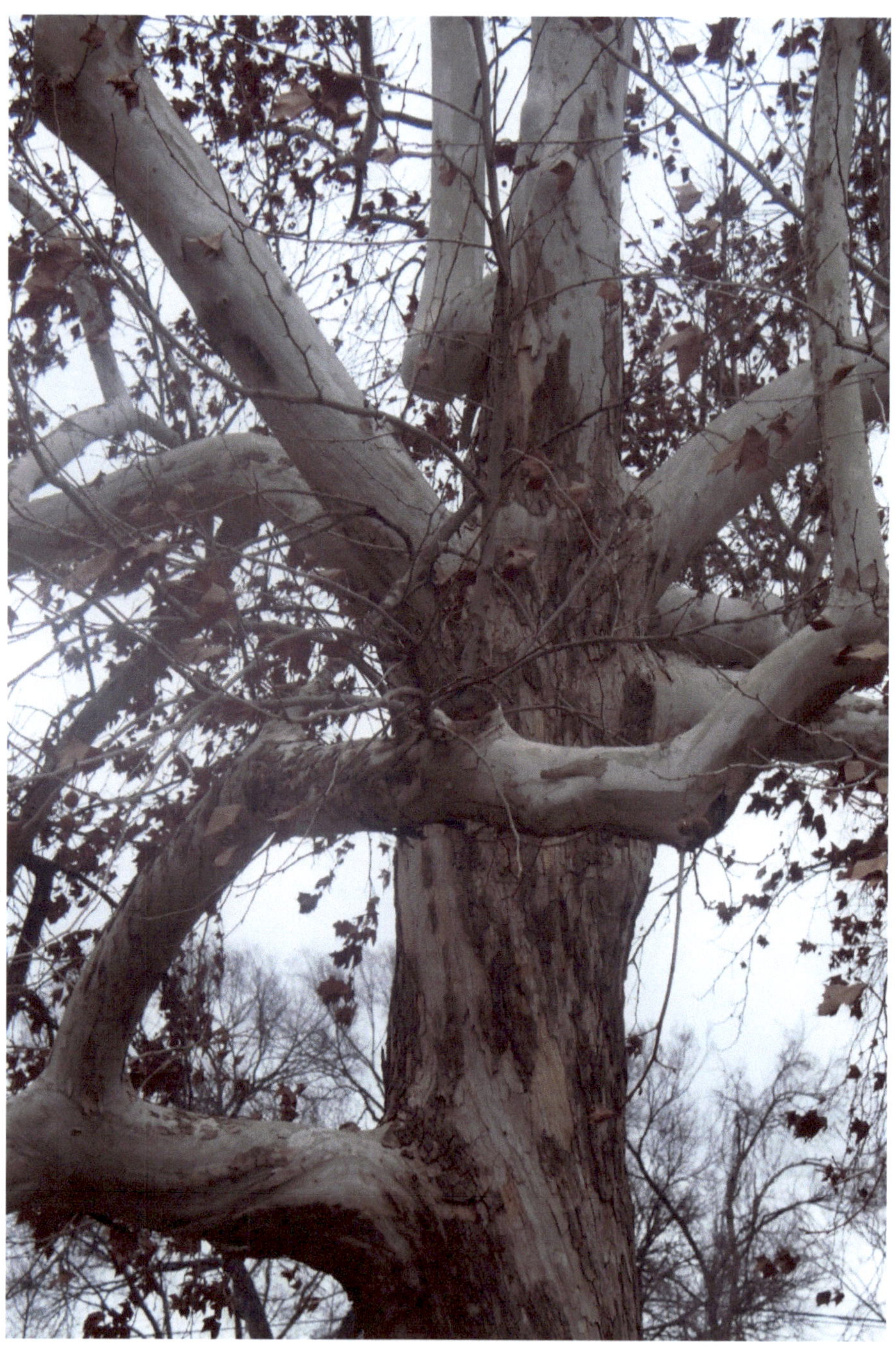

Natural Sculptures Revealed in Autumn

Just Thinking: A Time to Explore...Worldviews 3-b

Does the Bible present a legitimate world view? What kinds of world views are there? How do we know which to choose?

Theism
Deism
Naturalism
Nihilism
Existentialism
Eastern Pantheism
New Age Philosophy
Postmodernism

A worldview is a combination of assumptions about the way our world works.

The Bible is an example of Theism, because it is logical and faithful in these ways:

- It is believable.
    - Scientific and archeological evidence supports it.
    - Written over many years, the writers substantiate each other.
    - Continuity of doctrine remains in place throughout this literary work.
- It is appealing.
    - Logical explanations are given.
    - Emotional components are acknowledged and valued.
    - Factual evidence gives credence to what is written.
    - Personal experience proves its value.

A worldview can be justified or challenged. But eventually, it requires FAITH. Our natural instincts tell us that blind faith is dangerous. But a faith that is based on logical evidence and successful experience is worth the risk.

Explore the Bible:

- Genesis 1: 1-31 explains the creation of the world and of mankind.
- Psalms 4:1-03 shows an example of a successful prayer experience with God, the Creator of the universe.
- Genesis 3:1-13 introduces us to the concept of free will and the responsibilities/consequences that come with it.
- John 3:16-21 addresses the conquest of sin and the concept of eternal life.

Just Thinking: A Time to Explore…the Bible 4-a

How did we get the Bible? What does it consist of? Were there multiple writers? What about the Catholic Bible and the Mormon Bible?

- **The Bible**, as many people know it, contains a large collection of books and writers. It is divided into two segments, the Old Testament and the New Testament. Now the Old Testament alone is made up of 39 different books with as many writers. And it was written over a period of about 1,000 years. The New Testament contains 27 separate books and was written over a relatively shorter period of time. Altogether, they have survived over 2,000 years and have significantly affected the course of history. Surely, such a book deserves a close look.
- **The Catholic Bible** adds the Apocryphal writings. The word "apocrypha" means of questionable authenticity. Supposedly, they were written during the several hundred years between the writings of the Old Testament and those of the New Testament.
- **The Mormon Bible** adds The Book of Mormon. Members of the Church of Jesus Christ of Latter Day Saints believe it to be the writings of prophets living on the American continent from about 2200 BC to 421 AD. Written in a style similar to the King James Version, it was first published in 1830 by Joseph Smith.

I think it is significant, as well as comforting, to know that Mormons, Catholics, and Protestants all seem to agree that the contents of the King James Version of the Bible are the inspired words of God. To me, that seems like one proof of its scriptural validity. Using it as a resource, we are then free to discern for ourselves whether The Apocrypha and The Book of Mormon are a part of His Holy Scriptures or not. Thankfully, we can ask God, through prayer, for the wisdom to understand what He alone has inspired.

Explore the Bible:

- John 5:39 tells us that Jesus instructed the people to look for answers in the scriptures.
- James 1:05 reassures us that God will always give wisdom/discernment to whoever asks for it, if they trust Him to do so.
- Romans 4:23-24 connects Old Testament faith with New Testament faith.
- II Timothy 3:15-16 says the Old Testament scriptures are meant to make us wise and to lead us to the New Testament scriptures which explain the kind of faith in Jesus Christ that will make us eligible for eternal life in Heaven with God.

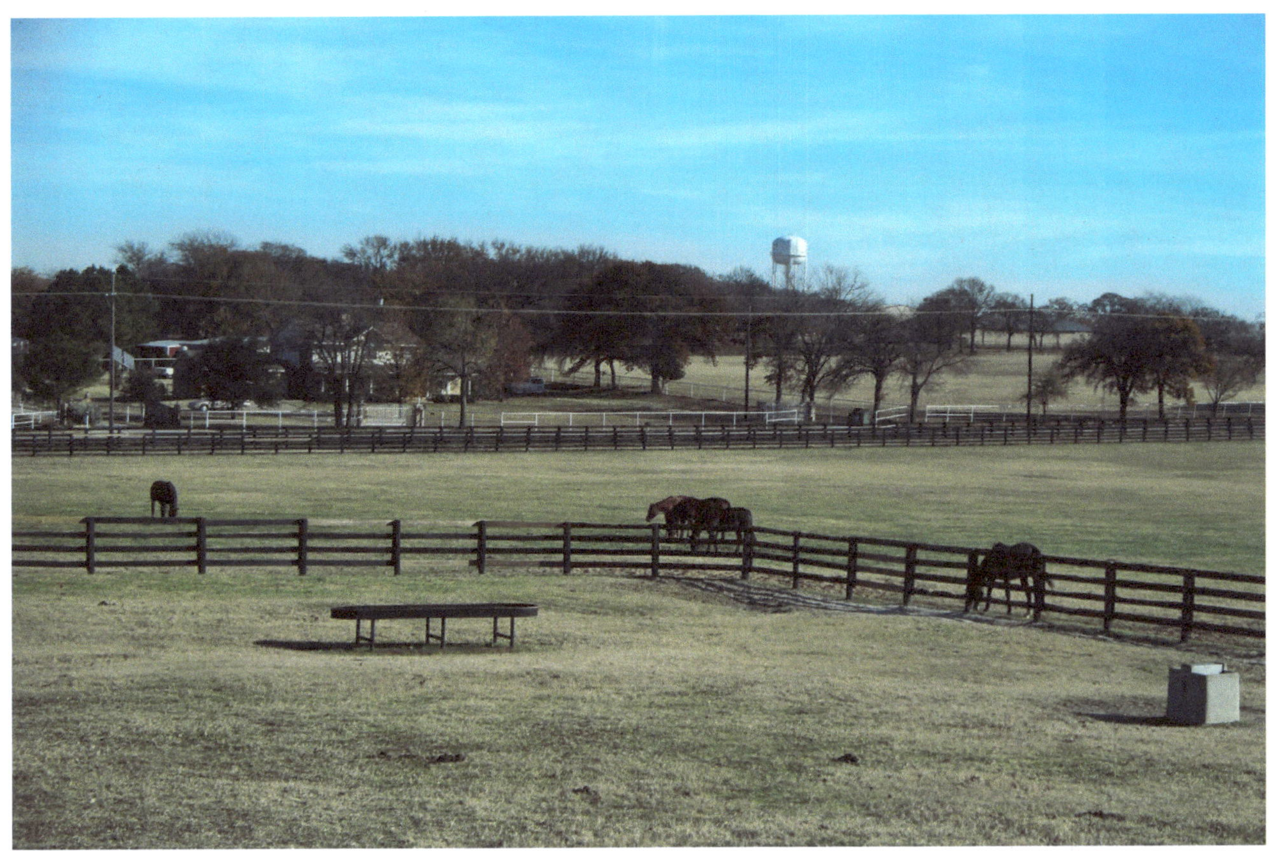

Beautiful Horse Country

Both my husband and I love horses. So we boarded a luxury coach for a full day of touring horse farms. Mild winters and sandy loam soil made this locale, as pictured above, ideal for the equine industry. In fact, the area boasted over 300 breeding and training facilities and about 40,000 horses. Now this was a great place to visit in order to observe modern day cowboys at work and at play.

The itinerary for this crisp fall day was a full one. First, we visited a ranch that specialized in Tennessee Walking Horses. Watching one majestic animal after another show off their unique walking style, it reminded me of a beauty pageant! Second, we educated ourselves at a farm that was known world-wide for their Arabian horses. Here we learned more than we ever wanted to know about modern horse breeding! Toward mid-day everyone was treated to a delicious chuck wagon lunch with all the trimmings. Guests filled their plates with beans and barbeque and then scrambled for the best seats. As many as possible ate their lunch seated on bales of hay arranged around a warm, crackling campfire! In the afternoon we spent the rest of the day touring the farm pictured above. It was known for being the home of two Kentucky Derby winners! With this fitting finale, we agreed that this had been a memorable day for any horse lover!

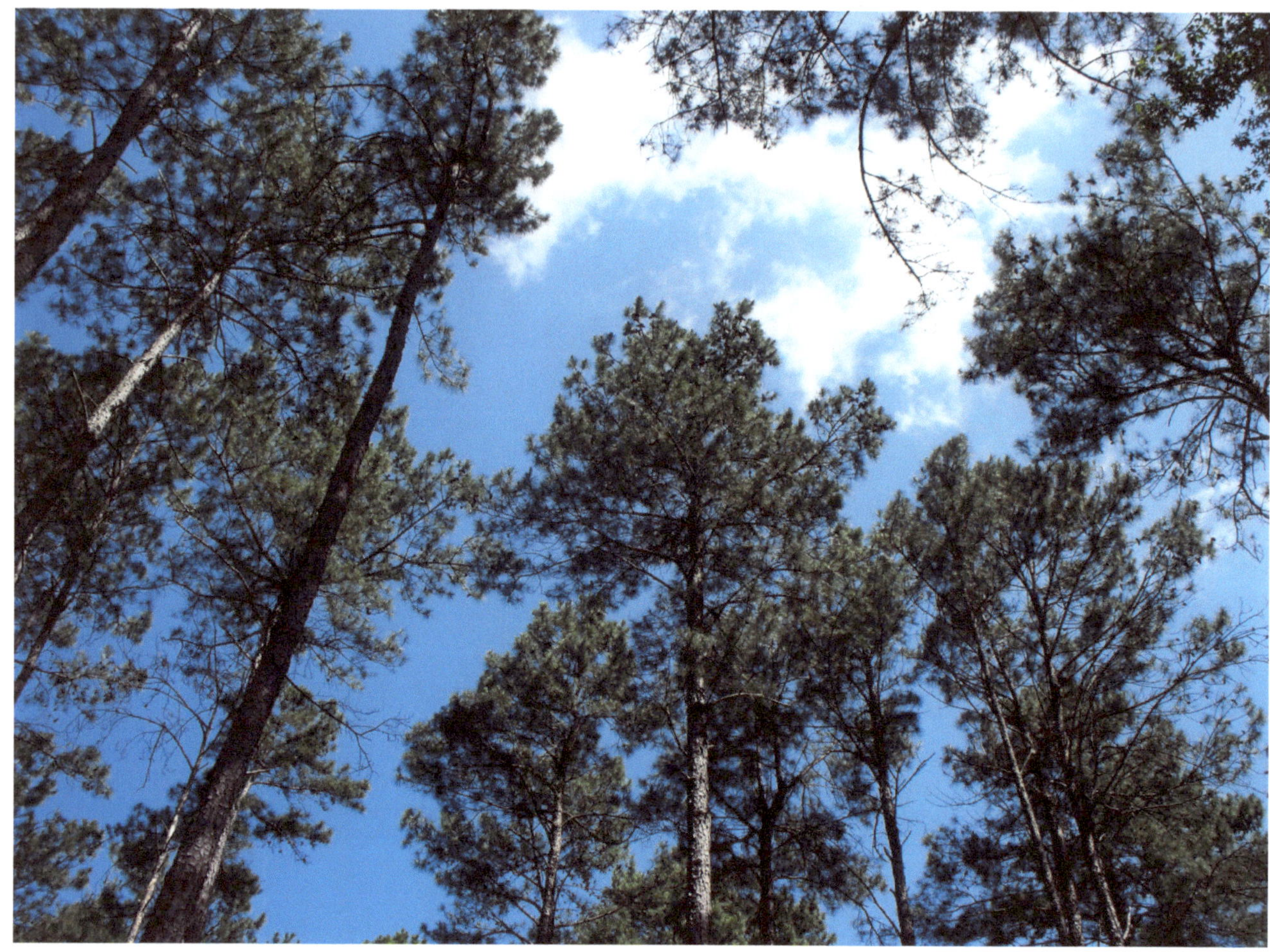

Just Look Up!

It is not uncommon for people to look up to the sky, when they think of God in Heaven. But WHERE in the heavens does He live? I doubt that we will ever know the answer to that question in this lifetime, but we CAN know what it is like for His spirit to make its home in our hearts.

When I was a tiny little girl, I had been to a Sunday School class and the topic for that day had been how Jesus can live in our hearts. When I came home, I asked, "Mommy, when I drink water, does Jesus get wet?" I do not remember this occasion, but I have enjoyed hearing about it a number of times over the years. I am sure my mother must have smiled and then explained that Jesus is not literally inside our hearts, but that if we put our faith in Him to save us from our sins, God's spirit will fill us with the assurance that we belong to Him and that He follows us wherever we go, so that we are never alone. We do not have to look UP to find God; we can feel His presence in our hearts.

Just Thinking: A Time to Explore…God

How do I know that God is real?

If so, what does He want with ME?

In ancient mythology, many different gods were worshiped. Each god represented something different in life---the god of fertility, of the harvest, of war, etc. They were each limited in their scope. But the Bible speaks of ONE omnipotent (all powerful) deity---a god powerful enough to create the sun, moon, and stars, as well as everything and every person on the face of the earth. When I look at the intricate design of the world, with everything in perfect balance, I think it makes sense to believe it was the work of ONE creator with His own master plan. And it is logical to think that the universe is too intricately designed to be just one accident after another. This was a god that was also omnipresent (ever-present), having existed from the beginning of time. And in addition, this was a deity that was omniscient (all-knowing), the source of all knowledge and all wisdom. This deity is called "God".

- Is God real or just a figment of the imagination? If we cannot see something with our own eyes, it can be hard to believe it is real. But, even though the wind cannot be seen, we know it is there, because we can hear it and feel it and we can see what it does. In the same way, we can know God is real. When we hear God's words and they ring true in our minds, we know He is real. When we feel His presence in our hearts, we know He is real. And when we see the things He does in our lives, we know He is real.
- What is God like? In fact, He is much like us in many ways. The Bible says He fashioned mankind after Himself. Just like us, He has emotions like love, joy, disappointment, anger, etc. He is the designer/creator of everything that people can feel and experience---curiosity, humor, pleasure, fear, sorrow, and even guilt.
- So, why did He create humans? He wanted a relationship with each and every one of us. Most human beings want children of their own that they can love, nurture and enjoy. If we were made in God's image, then it is not hard to imagine God wanting the same thing. Surely, that is why the Bible speaks of people as God's children.

Explore the Bible:

Genesis 1:01-31 states that God formed the heaven with the sun, moon, and stars along with the seas and the dry land. Then He made plants to fill the earth. Next, He created all living things like reptiles, birds, and animals. Lastly, He made mankind in His own image or likeness to rule over and subdue all that He had made.

Just Thinking: A Time to Explore...Heaven 6-a

What are the mysteries of Heaven?

Heaven is where God resides. There is so much that I do not know about Heaven, but I think the best thing about it, will be the opportunity to live in our Creator's magnificent presence forever. I would never want to even imagine what it would be like to exist for eternity without our loving Heavenly Father, God. That, alone, would be enough to convince me that I made the right choice when I accepted Jesus, God's son, as my personal savior from my sins. *The Bible makes it very clear, that we cannot experience everlasting life in Heaven unless we have made that choice.*

So what will Heaven be like?

- God will be there.
- There will be no sin.
- People will not marry.
- Rewards will be given out.

It will be wonderful to sit in God's presence. No one will harm anyone else there. Couples will not be bound to each other; instead, they will be able to concentrate on heavenly things, much like the angels in Heaven. Some people will have more honors/rewards than others, according to the way they lived their days on earth during their lifetime.

The Bible says that wherever our treasures are, THAT reflects where our hearts are. It is better to store up treasures/rewards in Heaven than to stockpile earthly possessions, because only heavenly treasures are lasting.

I do not know much about Heaven, but I am VERY sure that I will not be disappointed!

Explore the Bible:

- Matthew 5:34 says that God's throne is in Heaven.
- Matthew 22:30 explains that men and women will live like angels who do not marry.
- Matthew 6:9-13 tells us that God's will is done in Heaven.
- Revelations 2:23 speaks of being rewarded for good deeds.
- Revelations 2:26-29 talks about special privileges to be given out in Heaven.

Just Thinking: A Time to Marvel

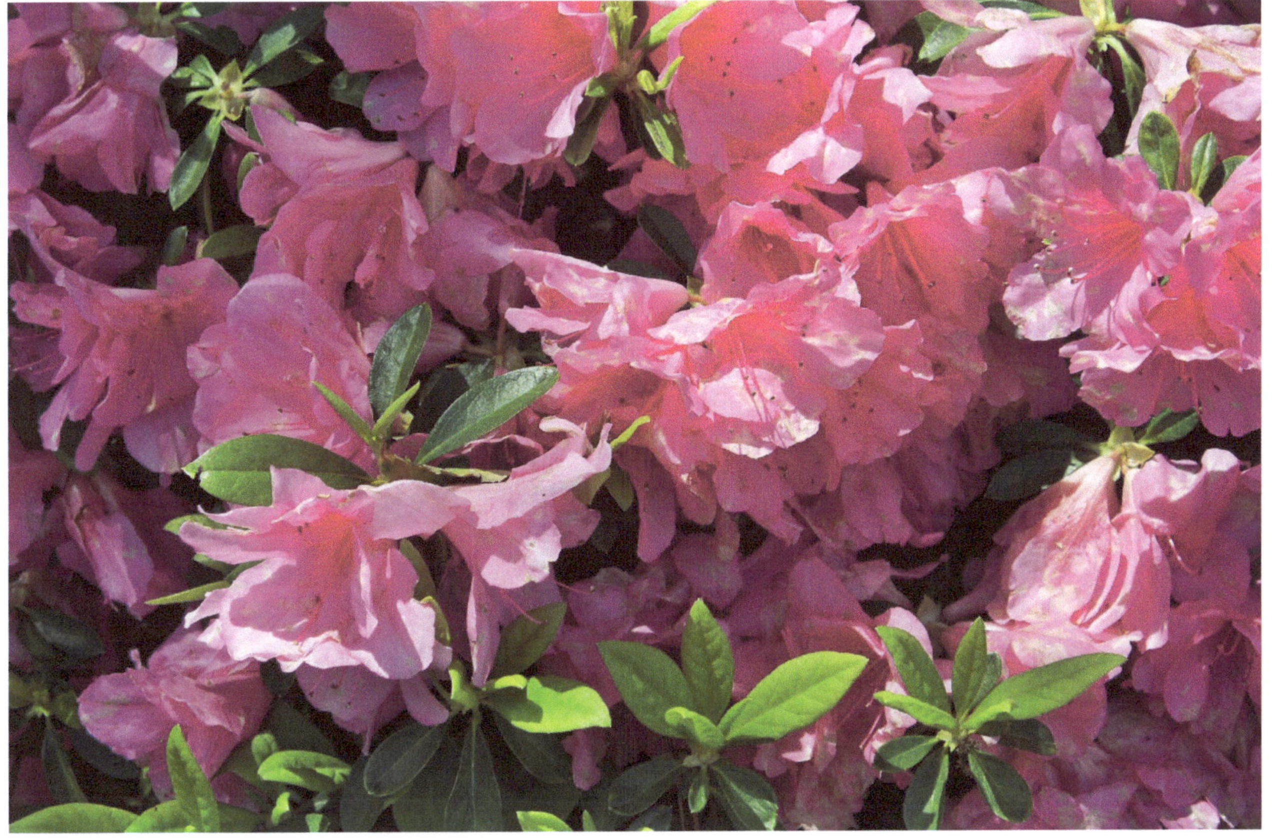

Are There Any Pink Azaleas in Heaven?

One of my favorite places to visit in the springtime is an azalea trail not too far from my childhood home. Somehow, it is so easy to miss out on the beauty and attractions close to where we live; taking our vacations far away somewhere else seems more enticing. It wasn't until my own children were grown that I finally discovered the joy of an azalea trail in my own home town. As my husband and I drove along the historic streets, we came to an area where we were allowed to stroll through the personal gardens of certain private properties. Not only were the flowers and canals breathtaking, but docents dressed in colorful antebellum costumes stood by, happy to adorn our photos with the charm of yesteryear. Finding azaleas of several different colors and hues, I was also amazed by how healthy and lush each plant appeared. As we walked along curving paths, from one yard to the next, we came across gazebos and patios placed in strategic areas, in such a way as to entice a weary visitor to come and just rest amongst the splendor there. Surely, gardens like these must be a tiny preview of what Heaven will be like. Now that is something to look forward to!

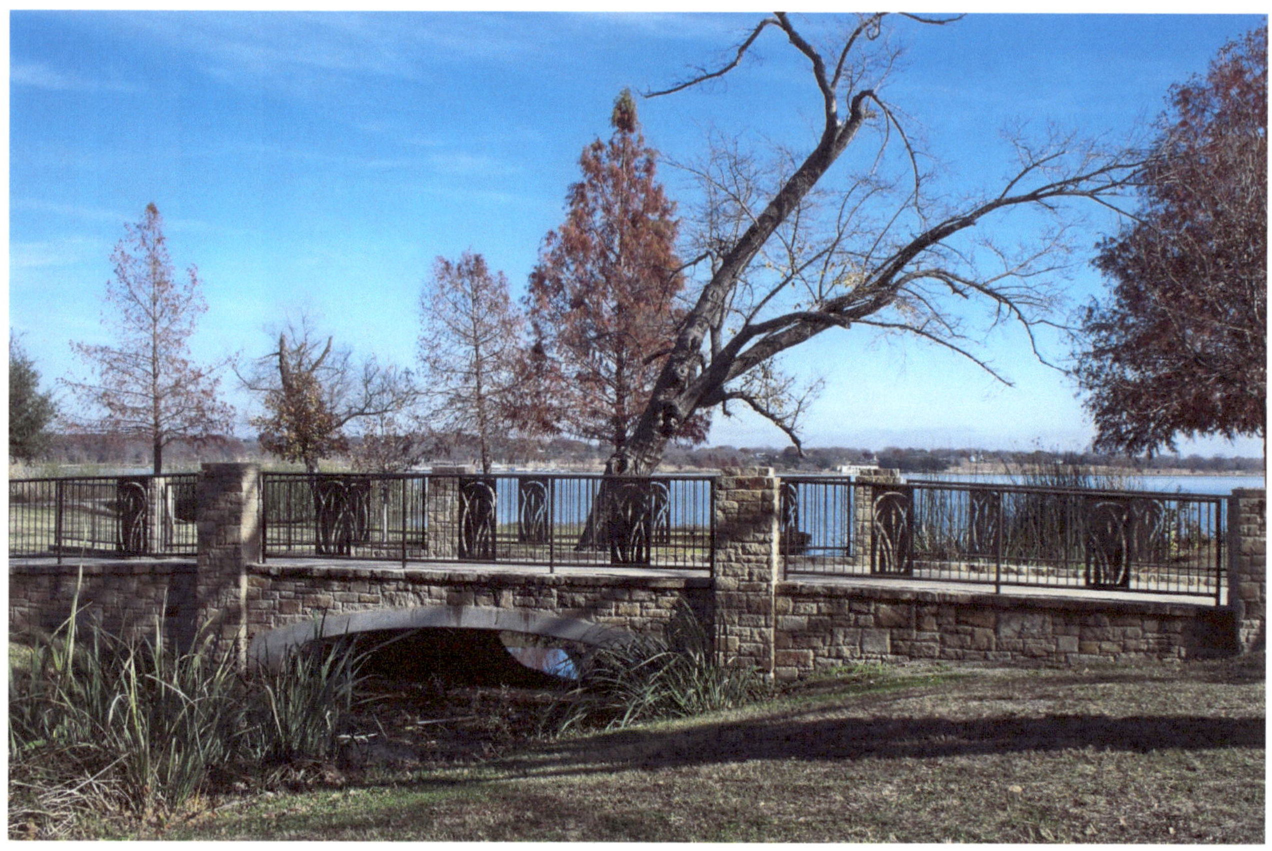

A Bridge to God

In the beginning, when God was sitting on His throne in Heaven, I sometimes wonder what He had in mind when He began to create the universe. A smile creeps onto my face as the thought occurs to me that it must have been something like designing a board game such as Monopoly or the Game of Life. I am certain that He could have created a game plan that would have had a fixed outcome. But when God gave people the freedom to choose whether or not they would trust Him in their daily lives and for their eternal safety, it became a great adventure---maybe the only thing that He did not plan out. Of course, the omnipotent God that He is, He would have been able to see into the future, knowing that people would not follow the perfect course that He had planned for them. He would know that their sin would form a huge chasm between them and Himself. They would need a safe bridge that would take them back to God. And that bridge is His only son, Jesus.

Just Thinking: A Time to Explore...Eternity

What might a salvation prayer look like?

Dear God,

I am ashamed of some of the things that I have done or thought or wished; I realize that I deserve to be punished. The Bible tells us that no one can spend eternity in Heaven with You unless their sins are forgiven/pardoned by You. But forgiveness comes at a high price, because the penalty for sin is death. However, You loved all people so much that You sent Your own innocent son, Jesus, to take the punishment for all their past, present, and future sins. Yes, Jesus died on the cross in MY place!

After Jesus' death on the cross, You brought Him back to life to live with You for all eternity. And You promised to do the same for everyone who accepts Jesus as their personal savior from their sins. Many people know this gift of salvation is available, but have not chosen to accept it; therefore, they will never experience the gift of eternal life. But I DO accept this free gift of salvation from my sins. Thank you!

I could never be good enough to earn this gift of eternal life, dear Heavenly Father. But I know it is right to show You my appreciation by devoting my life to honoring You. That means making it my goal to follow Your loving directions for my daily life, no longer being a slave to sinful living, which distresses You so. This is my way of thanking You for saving me from my sins. It is the way that I worship you each and every day.

I am offering this prayer to You, God, because Jesus' death on the cross for my sins gives me the great privilege of talking directly to You. Thank you so much! Amen.

Explore the Bible:

- Romans 5:12 tells us that all people have sinned.
- Romans 6:23 reminds us that the wages of sin is death.
- John 3:16-17 shows God's great love and explains what He did to save us from ourselves.
- Romans 6:6-14 teaches that we were once the slaves of our sinful nature.
- Romans 6:19-22 explains that the gift of salvation has freed us to live a richer life.
- Romans 12:1-2 instructs us to offer ourselves to God's service.

Just Thinking: A Time to Explore...Prayer

Have you ever wondered about prayer? What is it, exactly? Are there specific things that we are to pray about? How often can we pray? Do we have an example of how to pray? Are there limits on what we can expect when we pray?

Can God hear me when I pray silently?
Does He really understand every language in the world?
How can I know that God hears my prayer?

Prayer is a conversation with the Creator of the human race. He is called by the name of God, Lord, and Father, etc. It is very important to communicate with God. Some specific things that are appropriate to include in our prayers are:

Praise Thanksgiving Forgiveness Daily needs

No personal concern is off limits to bring to Him in prayer. God wants a daily relationship with you. This means talking to Him, telling Him how you feel, what you are afraid of, asking Him questions, etc. Language is not a barrier, because no words have to actually be spoken; He understands your thoughts and feelings, whether or not you have words to express them. If He was able to give you the ability to think and feel, then surely God also has the power to understand those thoughts and feelings without any words uttered. He wants us to pray frequently; after all, a relationship must be nurtured in order to thrive. It is the same way in our daily lives with friends, family, and co-workers; we must maintain regular dealings with them to keep the relationships strong and healthy. Fortunately, Jesus gave us an example of how to pray in the Lord's Prayer. We often do not have the things we desire in life simply because we have not asked for them OR when we have requested something that is not good for us OR when we have petitioned for something with a dishonorable motive in our heart. But we can know that God has heard our requests, because He loves us. He is no different than a parent who is happy to accommodate his child, as long as the request is not harmful to the child's welfare. God honors requests made in faith and He never makes promises that He does not keep.

Explore the Bible:

- I Thessalonians 5:17 teaches that we cannot pray too often.
- James 4: 2-3 says we do not have our desires because we have not asked for them or because we have asked for the wrong things.
- Romans 8:26-27 reassures us that God understands our prayers without words.
- Matthew 21:22 promises that requests made with faith, will be honored.
- Titus 1:02 informs us that God cannot lie.

Just Thinking: A Time to Marvel

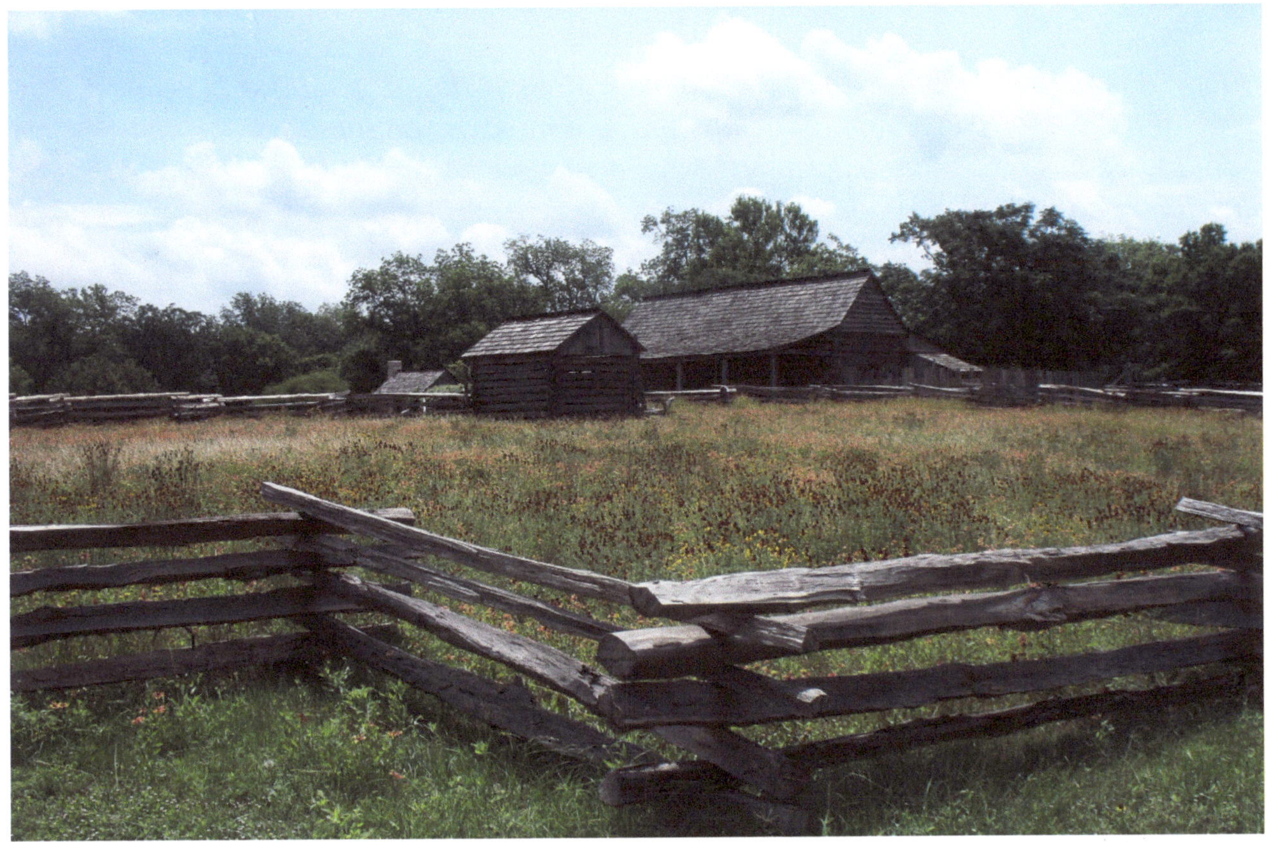

The Prairie in Spring Time

For the last several years my family has been celebrating all of the birthdays at once by planning a yearly week-end family activity. I am a great proponent of finding ways to manage stress; so, this idea appealed to me, because it would tremendously ease the challenge of finding presents for my nine grandchildren! And I was also anxious to emphasize quality family time over material gifts. Now I just set aside the amount of money I would have spent at birthday parties and apply that toward the total family gathering expenses. It is so much more pleasant this way!

We choose something different to do every year. In the photo above, you can see my favorite landscape on the public farm that we visited one year. This is a place where families get the chance to learn, first-hand, about farm life in the 1800s from docents clad in period-costumes. The children enjoyed helping to carry buckets of water and they even were allowed to wash clothes on an old-fashioned washboard. Several of them hung clothes out to dry on the outdoor clothesline, using wooden clothes pins. This was an educational and rewarding experience for us all. But the best part was just doing it TOGETHER!

Just Thinking: A Time to Explore...Solitude

When I take a few minutes at the beginning of each day to spend a little quiet time alone, it helps me to focus on the things that are most important to me for that day. In order to use this time more efficiently, I have designed the prayer below; it was modeled after the one that Jesus suggested to his disciples. Then I like to follow this prayer with a short passage from either the Bible or some other inspirational literature.

Dear God, I come to You, my Heavenly Father, in a reverent frame of mind. May Your will be done on earth, especially in my country, just like it is done in Heaven.

In the Bible, we are told not to worry about the future, so whatever my needs are for this day (physical or emotional or spiritual or otherwise), I ask You to supply those needs. I am taking You seriously, when the Bible says to take EVERYTHING to You in prayer.

The Bible instructs us to try to find out what Your will is, so please teach me today whatever You want me to know. Help me to promptly incorporate it into my daily life.

Please forgive me for any sins (wrongs) I may have committed and help me to quickly forgive those people who have sinned against me, because I am not perfect either.

I ask You to help me to do a good job of resisting evil today; I know You can do this because You are magnificent and full of power!

I can never pay You back for the eternal salvation from sin that You have freely given me (through Jesus' death and resurrection). Thank you for that gift; I accept it and I count on it. But I WOULD like to know what I can do for YOU today, God, as an act of thanksgiving and worship. Please help me do whatever that is.

Thank you for the many blessings/riches that You have already allowed me to enjoy in my life and for answering all these requests that I have made today in this prayer!

I present this prayer in Jesus' name (because of Him and in honor of Him). Amen.

Explore the Bible:

Matthew 6:05-13 tells us it is good to pray in a private place and also gives an example of how to pray.

Just Thinking: A Time to Marvel

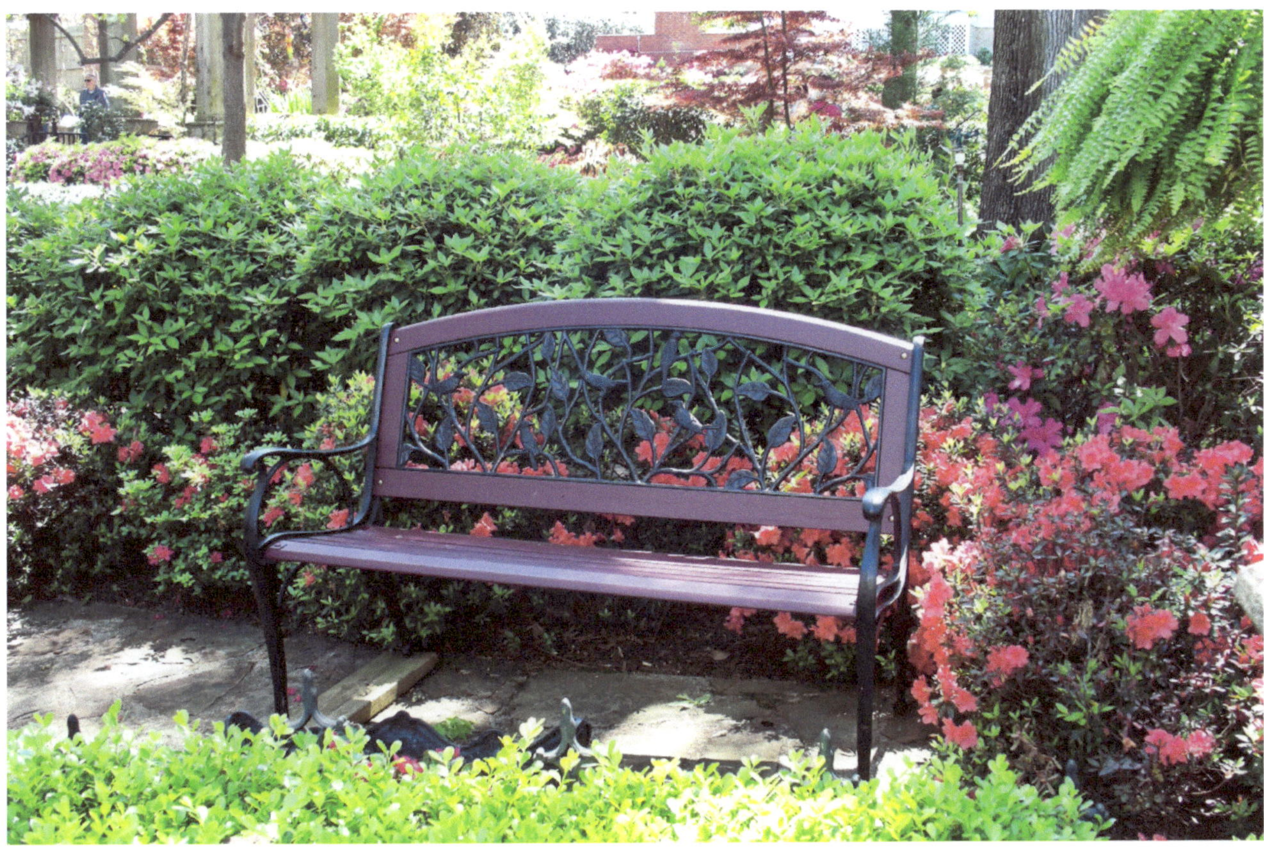

My Morning Oasis

I have found a way to actually look forward to my busy days. Instead of jumping out of bed at the last minute, I have learned to set the alarm for one hour earlier than it takes me to get ready for the day. (Of course, it helps to go to bed an hour earlier, provided there is nothing good to watch on television. Ha!). I stumble into the kitchen to begin my soothing morning ritual of putting coffee on to brew; somehow, I enjoy this mindless task, probably because it helps me ease into the day. Next, comes my predictable bowl of cereal and milk; and for a special treat, I sometimes add fresh fruit. By this time, the aroma of coffee is permeating the kitchen. So, I pour a cup, add some cream, and take it to the couch where I sit down and slowly savor my exotic liquid dessert! In the quiet of the morning, I just sit there, sipping and relaxing, thinking about nothing except the moment. Soon I become more aware of my surroundings and find myself marveling about things normally taken for granted; I hear the birds chirping outside, the clock chiming on the hour, and my husband beginning his own morning routine in the shower. Shortly thereafter, he joins me to share a second cup of coffee TOGETHER before the concerns of the day demand our attention. What a blissful way to start each new day!

Just Thinking: A Time to Marvel

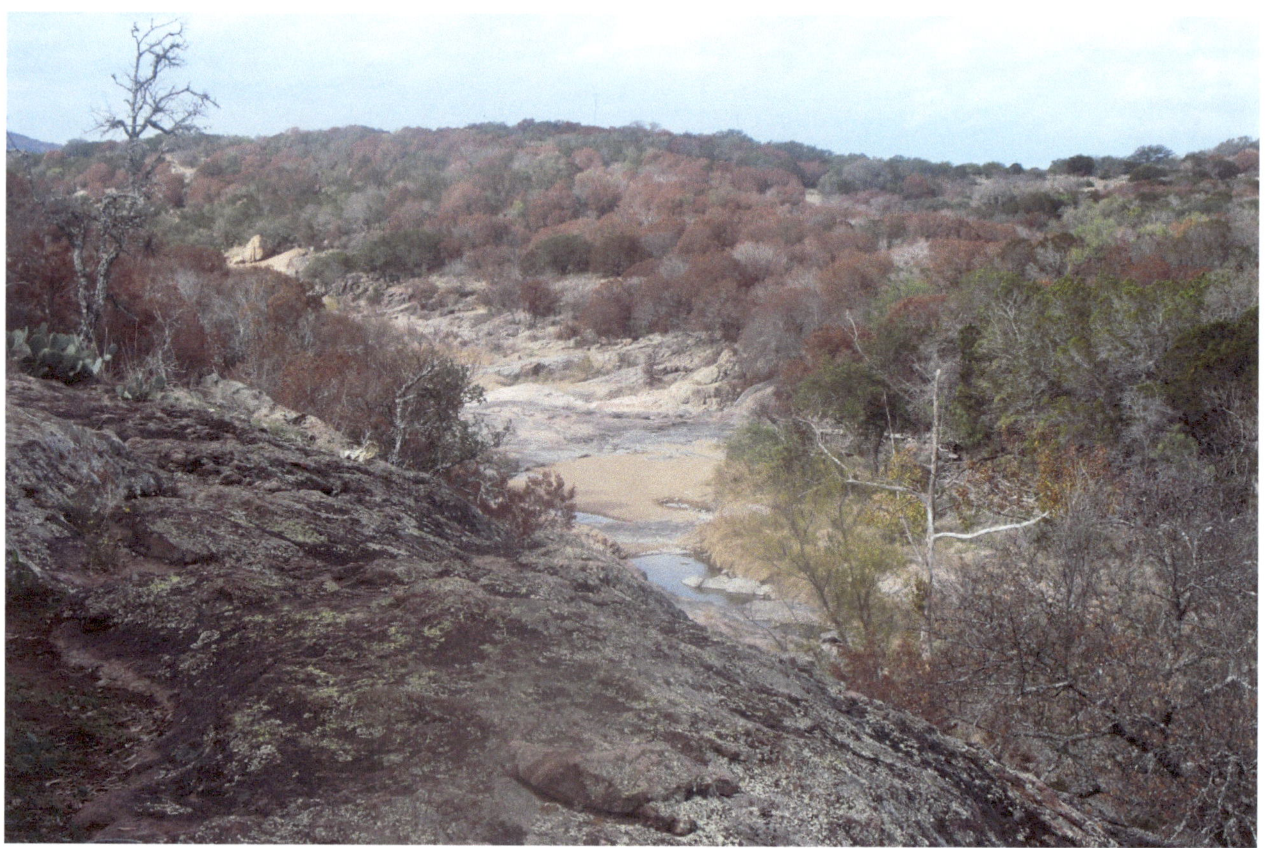

A New Perspective

One of my favorite things to do is to climb to a high spot and then look down to view what lies below, even when it requires that I master my natural fear of heights. Everything appears so tiny. Cars look like toys. And people seem to be scurrying around like ants. But the world itself appears larger than ever. It reassures me to see that there is still so much vacant land left on this earth for our use, providing we take good care of it and use it wisely.

When I am looking down from my high perch on a hillside or a mountain or a tall building, it seems like I would feel more powerful as I tower over seemingly diminutive objects below. But instead, I feel small, humbled by the expanse of the earth that is visible from this elevation and by the beauty that I see below me. It gives me a different view of nature and of life---a new perspective that overcomes me with gratefulness to be able to witness God's splendor from this vantage point. And it refreshes my spirit!

Just Thinking: A Time to Explore...Wealth 10-b

Is there anything wrong with being wealthy?

Will I be sorry if I spend all my time and effort in making money?

If I am content with what I have, does that mean I am lazy?

What is it that most people want more of?

Money Jewels Cars Property

Basically, I think we want security and treasures. But, as we all know, these things are not guaranteed to last. Our houses can burn down or go into foreclosure, 401-Ks can lose money and the stock market can crash, thieves can steal our cars, jewelry and electronics, and our Social Security and Medicare can diminish. We can accumulate wealth, but ultimately, our true source of security rests in God's hands.

The Bible teaches that having money is essential for our daily needs. In fact, we are urged to work enough for our own needs, as well as to have some left over to share with others who are less fortunate than ourselves. But God does not want us to be so consumed with attaining wealth that we resort to dishonorable behavior or to neglect other important things in our lives, in our search to become richer or more secure. How many of us have heard older people wishing they had spent more time with their loved ones, instead of spending too many of their waking hours in the pursuit of stock-piling money or possessions? Learning to be more content with what we have can be a great relief as well as a blessing!

Our Creator does give us many wonderful things to enjoy in life; riches are not sinful. But the Bible encourages us to balance our lives by putting first things first; God knows that riches will not give us lasting peace or true happiness. Surely our most valuable and secure treasures are to be found in a personal relationship with Him.

Explore the Bible:

- Matthew 6:19-24 reminds us that our lives will reveal where our treasures are.
- I Timothy 6:7-10 shows us that loving money too much can ruin a person.
- I Timothy 6:17-19 explains that God wants us to have many things to enjoy, but to realize that true security is found in Him, not in material things.
- Titus 3:14 tells us to not to be lazy, so that we can earn money for daily needs.
- Hebrews 13:5-6 urges us not to live for money, being content with what we have.

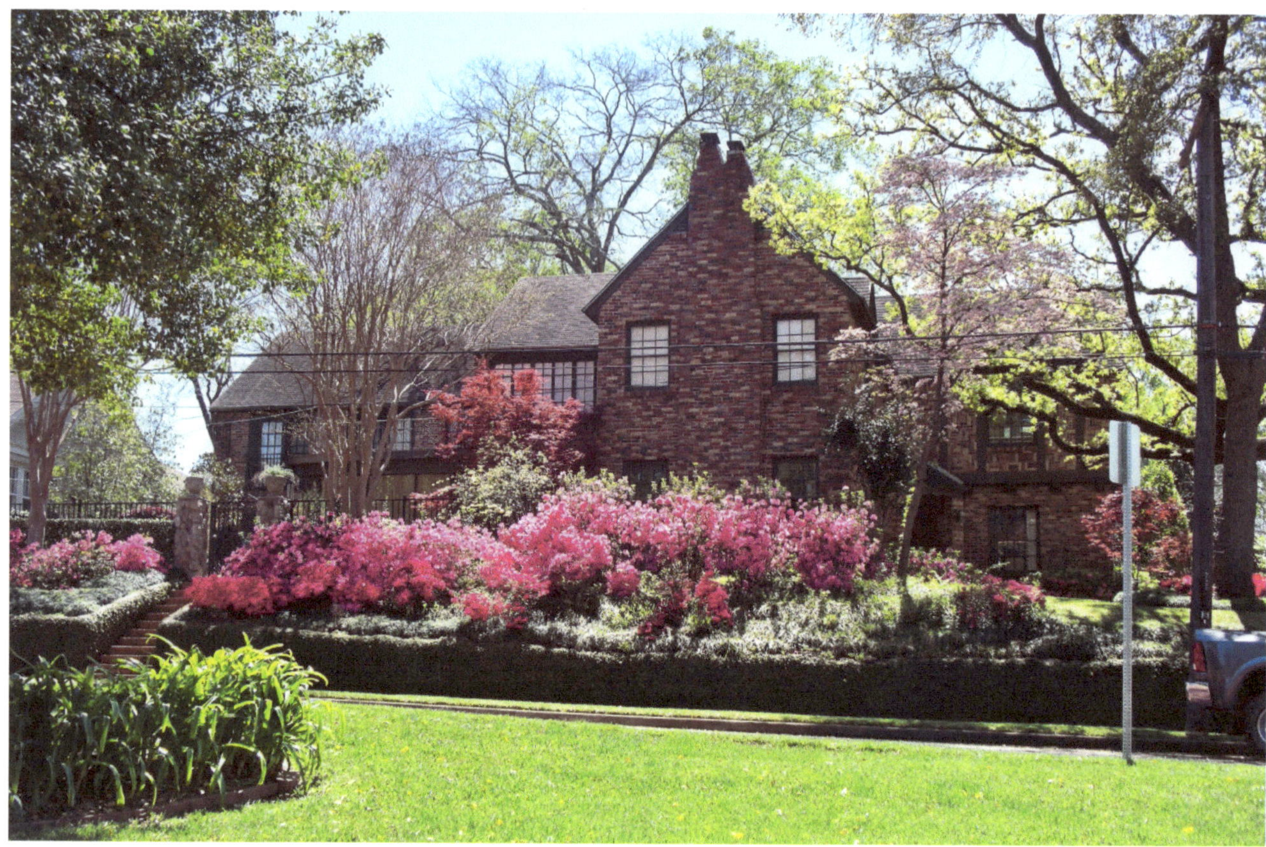

Memories Nourish Us

I had an unexpectedly pleasant experience when I visited my dad's grave site for the first time. Not looking forward to the occasion, yet strangely drawn to it, I was anxious to see what his head stone would look like. As I focused on the beauty of its color and design and read the elegant script on its highly polished surface (naming his wife and each of his children), I immediately sensed a peace come over me; it felt like our whole family was gathered at the monument, for all posterity to know that we belonged to each other as a family unit. It was a warm, cozy feeling; my body and psyche could "feel" the realization that this is not a grave site. Our loved one is not really there. Instead, it is a MEMORIAL site---a testimony to a person's life. At a grave site, you mourn the person's death, but at a memorial site, you celebrate their life! It is a place to remember the good times---much like looking through scrapbook pages, enjoying all over again the experiences that have been captured on film OR like watching a favorite movie many times over OR re-reading a special book. Even though we already know how the stories will turn out, it does not keep us from relishing the tale all over again. Our lives are a story that we all know will someday end. But ENJOYMENT of our loved one's life can last as long as we allow it to continue nourishing us through our memories!

Just Thinking: A Time to Explore…Giving

Is it MY fault that there are so many needy people?

It is overwhelming!

The Bible encourages us to be good stewards of our money. This is what being a good steward might look like:

- Giving according to our financial ability
- Working hard enough to have something to spare for helping others
- Giving cheerfully
- Offering a gift of money as a form of worship
- Giving as a way to thank God for our blessings
- Making it a priority to give on a regular basis

One of my favorite childhood memories was my dad's view on giving to worthy causes, even if it hurts a little. He said that God will take care of our own needs when we honor Him by giving tithes and offerings. It was all about having the proper priorities in our lives. I love the idea that God wants us to step out in faith, maybe giving a little more than is comfortable, and knowing that He honors/ rewards that degree of commitment.

I have come to love the part of the church service when offerings are taken. It actually FEELS like a time of worship, when I give my money, because it is like I am saying "thank you" for all the riches that I have been given. No, giving tithes and special offerings are not a chore for me; instead, they have become a blessing!

Explore the Bible:

- Titus 3:14 teaches us to work to provide our own necessities.
- Hebrews 13:16 reminds us to share whatever we have with others.
- I Corinthians 16:02 states we are to give according to our financial ability.
- 2 Corinthians 8:13-14 explains that God does not ask for what we do not have to give.
- 2 Corinthians 9:6-15 urges us to give cheerfully to good causes, not out of compulsion.
- Luke 12:29-31 reassures us that when we put first things first, that the rest will come to us.

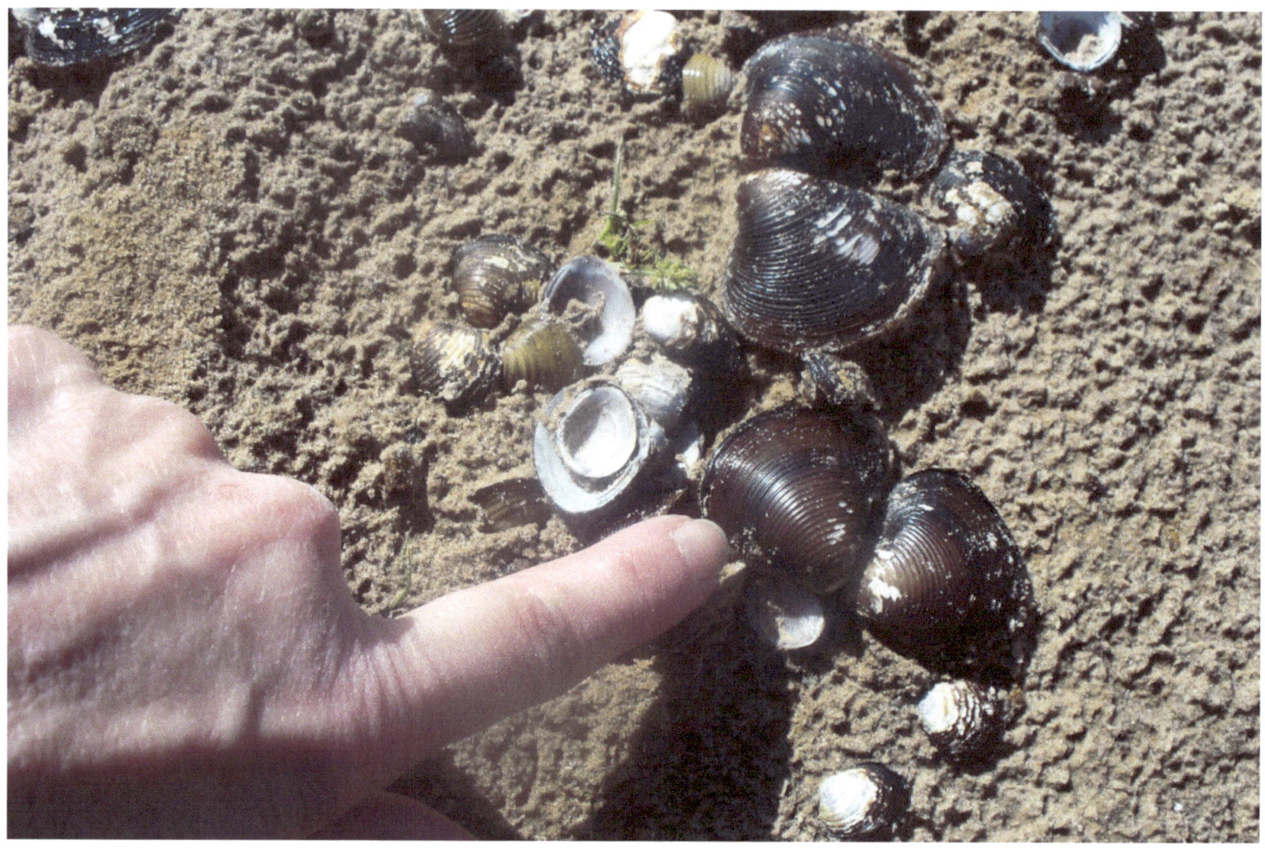

Shells on the Lake Shore

Camping is a forever changing experience. Over the last few years, my husband and I have tent-camped an average of five times per year. These trips may last anywhere from one night to five or six nights. Sometimes we go back to the same park, but usually stay at a different site or better yet, during a different season of the year. We also like to camp in a variety of states when the opportunity arises. One might think that all camping trips are the same, but I have learned to purposely look for the differences in each one. Every trip has its own story to be told. On one particular occasion, I was intrigued by the low lake level during a time of drought; until then, I had not noticed the sand and the shells you see me pointing to in the photo above. How tiny some of them were! They were like clusters of delicate gems sparkling up at me from their home on the beach floor. On a previous trip, at this same park, we woke up to find perfect little paw prints made of sand, standing out against the backdrop of the dark green fabric of a camp chair; it was obvious that raccoons had visited during the night! Yes, a person might think that camping would become boring after a while, but I have found that each individual experience has its own special memories, making it uniquely different from the rest!

Just Thinking: A Time to Explore…Joy

Do you ever feel overburdened with rules and regulations, guidelines and protocols, laws and other restrictions? Are you constantly being told "No" or "Wait"? Do you feel like you cannot live your own life freely? Are you full of resentment and stress because these things leave you very little "wiggle room" and joy in your life? Does it seem like God stands in the way of your personal enjoyment?

Is it God's mission to make me miserable?
Does He want to embarrass me?
Will He ruin my personal life?

I think most people, at some time or another, secretly have these kinds of thoughts. That is normal. But it is "self-talk" like this that will direct your actions. So, it is helpful to make sure you are telling yourself the truth… the WHOLE truth!

When you are tempted to pursue a pleasure that is not pleasing to God, try to remember that He is NOT trying to take away your happiness; after all, He is the original creator of pleasure! God just wants to ADD to the riches in your life. Consider trusting Him until you understand His purpose. Meanwhile, try to see what that plan is; ask Him for understanding. Let Him speak to your heart about it. I always find that living according to His direction is no burden, once I understand what God has in mind. Then I feel free to follow Him with joy and gladness!

Every "no" or every "wait" that God gives you is paving the way toward a wonderful "yes" that He has in store for you.

Explore the Bible:

- I Timothy 6:17 states that God gives us an abundance of things to enjoy.
- James 1:17 explains that everything good comes from Heaven.
- Luke 11:13 reminds us that just as parents give good gifts to their children, God is even more willing and capable of providing His people with desirable things.
- I John 5:03 teaches that our Heavenly Father's commandments are not meant to be a source of grief.
- Ephesians 5:17 warns us that it is foolish to be ignorant of what the Lord's will is.
- James 1:05 promises that God gives wisdom to those who ask Him for it.

Just Thinking: A Time to Marvel

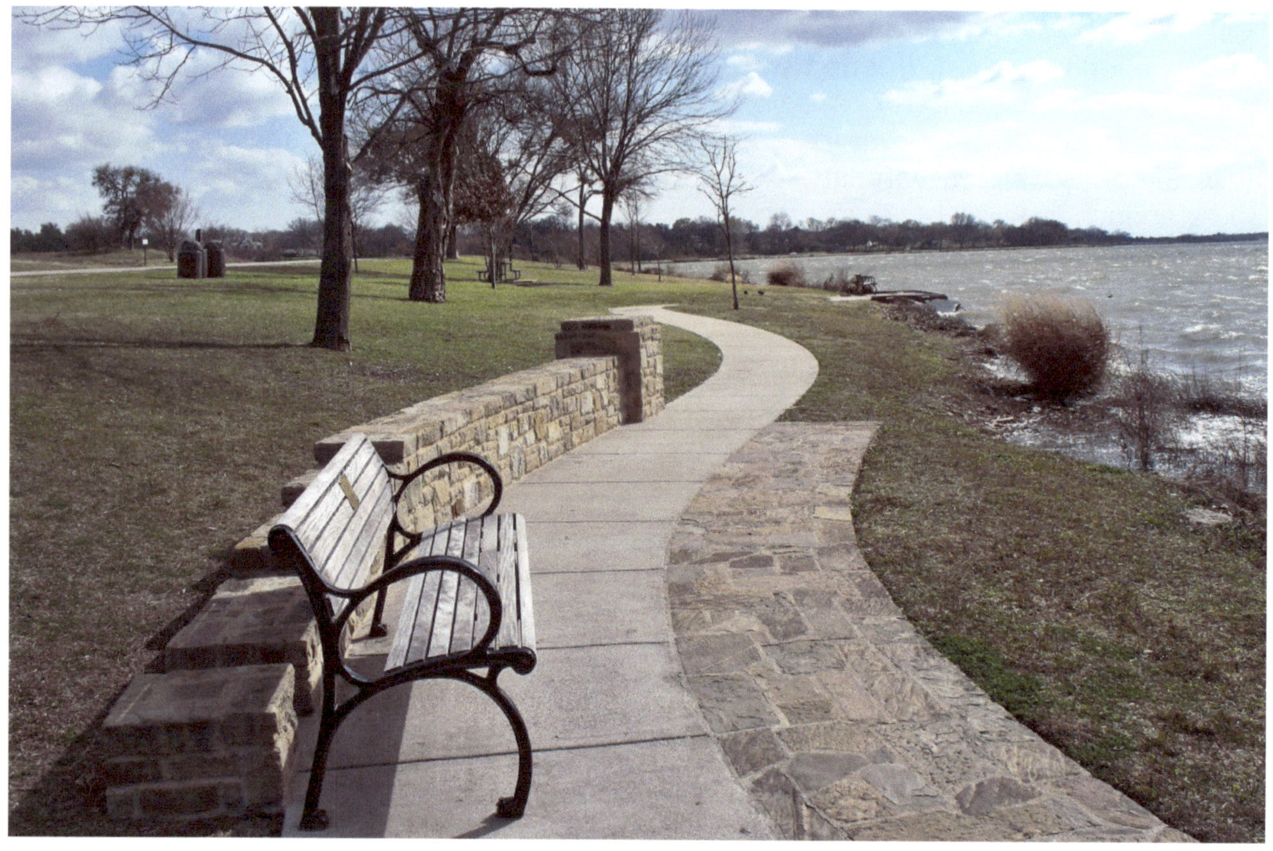

The Gift of a Sincere Compliment

It never wears down or runs out

Always fits

Is personalized

Cannot be lost or stolen

Is not outdated

Nourishes the receiver

And

Has a way of coming back

To the giver!

WORDS MAKE A DIFFERENCE!

Just Thinking: A Time to Explore...Words 13-b

Gossip Boasting

Slander/Lies Flippant Talk Coarse Expressions

One lesson that I have learned is that I may have the "right" to say something harsh, but instead, I can choose to say what is actually helpful to the situation.

Another thing I have realized is the importance of never saying something I don't really mean in the heat of the moment. What a terrible shame when words that I don't even mean do damage!

According to the Bible, the way we speak is very important, because our words are a direct reflection of what is in our hearts. How pleasant it is to be around a person who is in control of what he/she has to say!

Explore the Bible:

- James 1:26 says that religious people must have control over what they say.
- Titus 2:03 instructs us not to be scandal-mongers; this passage refers to people who participate in malicious gossip/rumors about other people.
- James 4:13-17 discusses the issues of arrogance and boasting/bragging.
- I Corinthians 6:9-11 states that slanderers are not pleasing to God.
- Ephesians 4:25 tells us to speak truthfully to each other. This is an example of trustworthiness.
- Ephesians 4:29-31 instructs us to say only things that are helpful/therapeutic, instead of indulging in angry shouting or cursing (irreverent speech or wishing harm to another).
- Proverbs 15:01-02 reminds us that a soft answer dissipates anger while a sharp response only stirs it up.
- Ephesians 5:04 explains that coarse talk (rough/crude), stupid talk, or flippant talk (not appropriately serious) is not what God has in mind.

WORDS ARE POWERFUL!

Just Thinking: A Time to Explore...Resentment 14-a

Has anyone ever stolen from you?

Were you bullied in the past?

Have you been wounded emotionally?

Resentment is defined as a feeling of annoyance (irritation or anger). As it grows, it becomes a grudge and then expands into hatred; resentment easily consumes the unsuspecting person. These emotions have been the reason for countless wars, feuds, lost jobs, damaged relationships and broken marriages. They are toxic feelings for the person who holds on to them. Unfortunately, resentment, grudges and hatred do the most harm of all to the one who nourishes them, not to the person who caused them.

I can think of a number of reasons for releasing yourself from the ugly clutches of resentment and its byproducts:

- To free yourself from the past so that you can go on with the good things in life
- To clear your mind and emotions to make room for more constructive endeavors
- To prevent your offender from continuing to harm you
- To find healing from hurtful relationships

Hanging on to resentments is a choice. When we choose to allow mistreatment to consume us, then it could be that we have elected not to forgive. Maybe we are waiting for an apology or justice or even for revenge. **But the truth is that we remain a victim until we have forgiven.** Fortunately, there is no need to wait. We can still forgive, even if the offender is not sorry. How? We can follow God's example. He forgave us of our sins even before we were sorry for them, by considering our NEEDS to be more important than the JUSTICE that we deserved. For an example of HOW to forgive, consider the woman who was finally able to forgive her rapist when she became sorrier for him than for herself.

God wants us to forgive each other. When we consider how God forgave sinners like US, how can we justify it when one sinner deprives another sinner of forgiveness?

Explore the Bible:

- Ephesians 4:32 reminds us to forgive each other, just as God forgave us.
- John 3: 16-17 explains that God sent His son, Jesus, to save the world, not to judge the world. He put our needs above justice.
- Luke 17:04 instructs us to keep on forgiving as many times as needed.

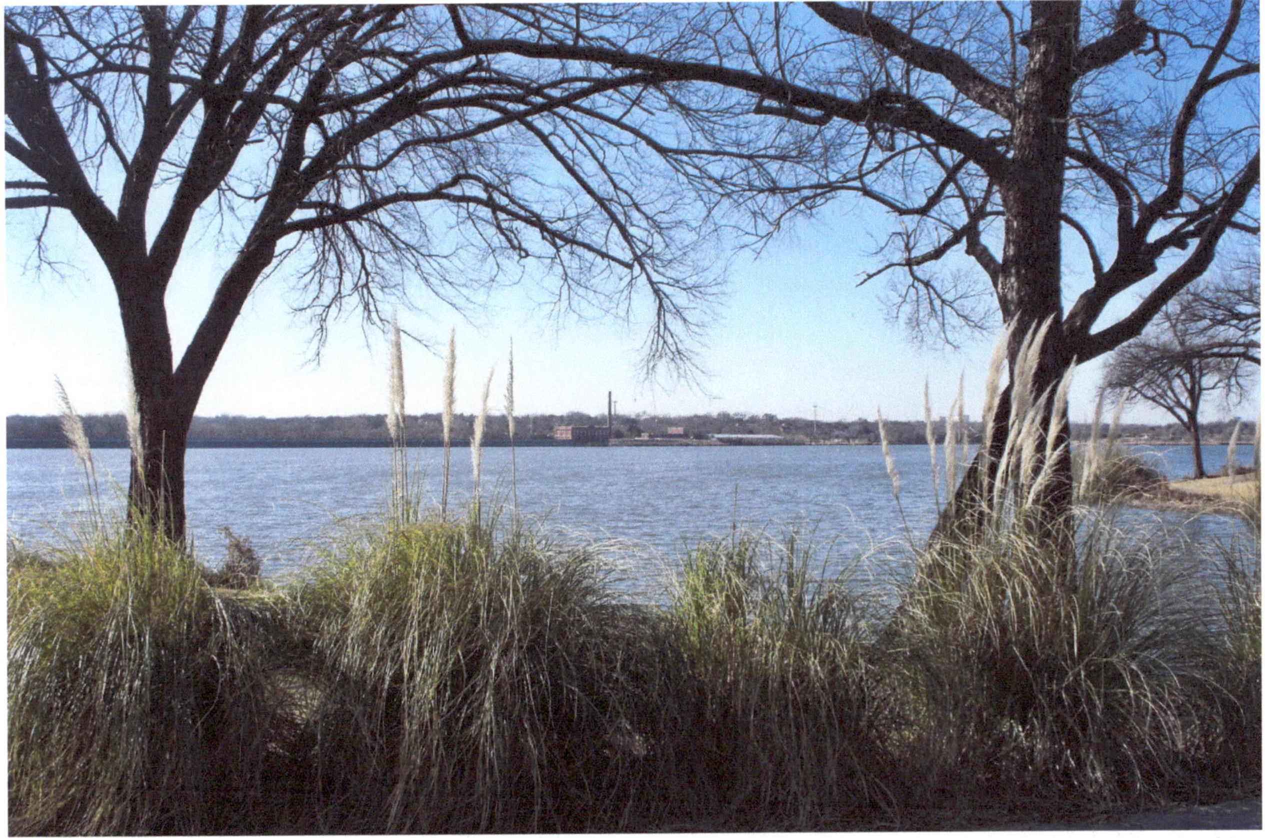

Nothing Drab About Autumn

Last fall I began taking my exercise routine to the outdoors. My first thought was that it was a shame to start during the drab days of autumn. Somehow, I was thinking that the bright colors of spring or summer would be more beautiful than the browns and grays of fall in my part of the country. But as I walked for an hour around the city lake, it became obvious that even New England's autumn foliage would be challenged by the shades of green, gold, cream, orange, brown and rust that decorated my own home area.

On my next walk at the lake, I took my camera. During the first half of the hike, I concentrated on the scenery. Even the trees that were colorless, like those in the photo above, were intriguing by the way they framed the picture. Never did I imagine that lush green grasses and cream-colored reeds, taller than my own five foot stature, as shown here, would grace my exercise path. It was hard to decide what I enjoyed the most...the sensation of crisp fall air, the sights and sounds of the outdoors, the energizing brisk walk or the vibrant colors of the foliage that I was able to capture on film. No, there was nothing drab about autumn in THIS neck of the woods!

Just Thinking: A Time to Explore…Modesty

What is modesty?

How does it affect MY life in today's world?

Nudity was not a problem for God in the very beginning; after all, could God create something sinful? I think not. To this day, infants come into the world naked. He created female sex organs to nurse infants and male sex organs to produce offspring; these are obviously worthwhile and honorable body parts. But as soon as they first sinned, God made it known to the married couple, Adam and Eve, that parts of the human body were to be covered. God was obviously setting a precedent that would demonstrate the special honor that is bestowed upon our naked bodies.

The Bible never really tells us exactly what or how much of the body is to be covered. But in the New Testament we ARE clearly instructed not to be lewd. By definition the word "lewd" means "vulgar". It appears that God leaves it up to our own reasonable judgment to determine exactly what is lewd or vulgar. It could be that what is indecent in one situation would not be vulgar/lewd in another. For example, bathing, childbirth, breast feeding, diaper changing, medical attention, etc. are all examples of partial or full nudity that are not particularly sexually oriented even though sexual organs may be exposed.

The misuse of the naked body IS sinful. Since God clothed both the man and the woman, it is apparent that modesty applies to both sexes. Lewdness or indecency has to do with dress or actions or words that are prone to entice sexual arousal in a situation that is not acceptable by God, which means outside the sanctity of marriage.

Now sexual intercourse between a husband and wife is NOT considered to be lewd or vulgar; in fact, the Bible teaches that our natural sexual urges are honorable within the confines of marriage. The Bible considers a married couple to be "one body" and sexual union is an example of that oneness. In God's plan, sexual activity of any sort is an EXCLUSIVE benefit meant for the man and woman who have entered together into the highly esteemed institution of marriage. It seems appropriate, to me, that such a couple should be rewarded in such a unique and beautiful way!

Explore the Bible:

- Genesis 2 & 3 tells about Adam and Eve realizing that they were naked.
- Mark 7: 21-23 says that lasciviousness (lewdness/indecency) is wrong.
- I Corinthians 6:13-20 explains how pre-marital sex is dishonorable.
- Hebrews 13:04 teaches that God is exceedingly displeased with pre-marital and extra-marital sexual activity.

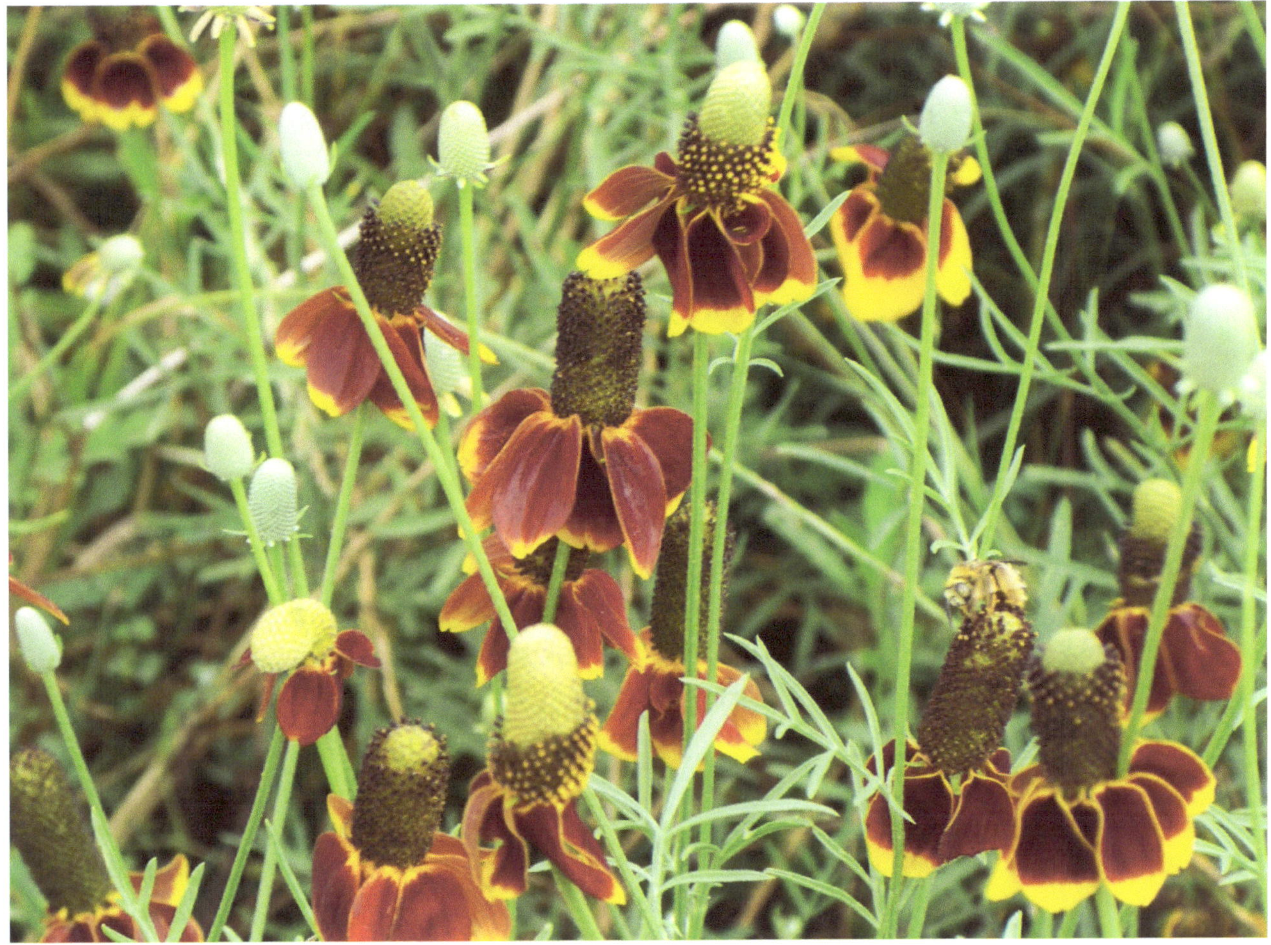

Nature at Its Best

Like the beautiful wild flowers pictured above, I think marriage was created out of the mind's eye of God. It united a man and a woman as life partners. Each one belonged to the other and to no one else. It was an exclusive relationship, in which pleural wives or multiple husbands were not the plan. It could be both romantic, as well as the ultimate business merger. It was the platform from which the human race would perpetuate itself. It would be the building block of strong nations. And the Bible tells us that marriage was meant to last for a lifetime.

Speaking of modesty, I once heard it said that nature is a good thing, but it is at its best when it is tamed a little. Modesty tames our naturally naked state in order to honor a very special commitment---marriage. I think our Creator knew that without modesty and sexual limits, we would not really understand the significance of the extra-ordinary and beautiful relationship that He meant for marriage to be.

Just Thinking: A Time to Explore...Family

What is the role of the husband?

Where does the wife fit into the picture?

How are children to be treated?

The family unit was created by God. It was not meant to be just a group of people of various ages living in the same household. There was a type of structure under which it was to exist. If you really take time to think about it, the design resembled a business plan. Visualize the husband and wife as members of God's executive committee, each having his/her own equally important responsibilities. And view their children as their precious charges. In the business world, it is commonly accepted that a company cannot be effective or successful without a hierarchy to direct the business toward a secure future. Likewise, the husband was to take the role of the head of the family, with the obligation of safeguarding its welfare. His supervisory style was to be that of a servant leader of his team rather than a harsh taskmaster. And the wife was to respect her husband's vital leadership role, while becoming the very life-blood of the corporation as his trustworthy advisor, executive assistant, business partner, etc. They were to be a team, collaborating together to reach their goal---a sound outcome on their investment in their marriage and their children's future. As parents, they were instructed to use every opportunity to teach wholesome principles to their offspring and to be ready to enforce reasonable discipline when necessary. I am sure God was aware that it could be tempting to abuse parental authority; therefore, parents were instructed not to exasperate their young charges. Surely, the family unit was one of God's most magnificent creations, because it has a unique power to be the backbone of the community, the nation, and even the world!

Explore the Bible:

- I Peter 3:07 instructs husbands to respect their wives, because they share in the gift of life together.
- Colossians 3:18-22 directs husbands to lead the family without being harsh.
- Ephesians 5:21-24 tells wives that they are to respectfully consider the husband as the head of the family.
- Ephesians 6:1-4 admonishes parents to teach and discipline their children without causing undue resentment.

Just Thinking: A Time to Marvel

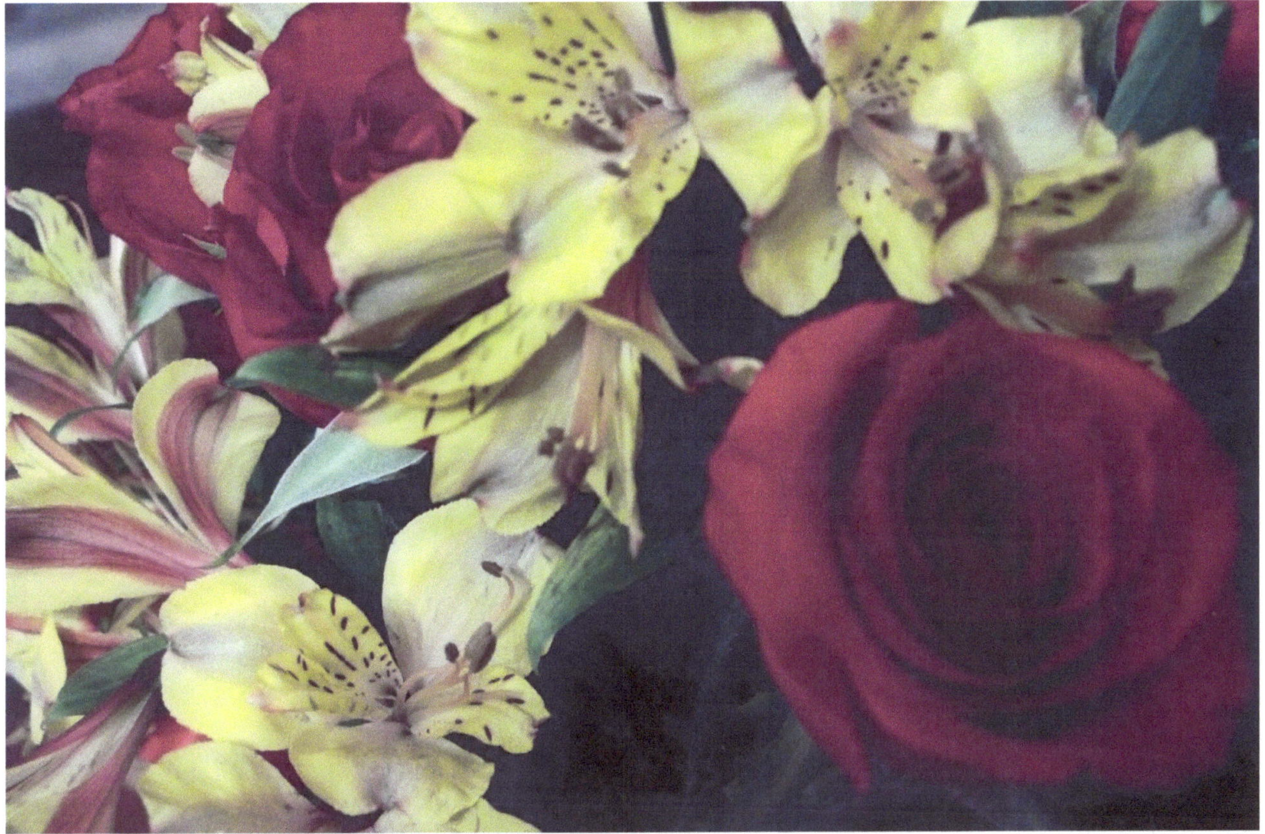

Motherhood-Past and Present

Until after the birth of my first child, I thought motherhood would be rather instinctual. I believed all the aspects of care, discipline and guidance would come with relatively little effort. But immediately after my daughter's birth, that assurance began to fade.

The process really began the first time I was left alone with my newborn. It was absolutely terrifying to suddenly realize how alien and helpless that little bundle of warmth was! As the first few months passed, I started to realize that motherly instinct is not an automatic storehouse of knowledge, as much as it is an emerging desire to become adept at this new role. So, I began to read literature on infants, listening and observing other mothers, and experimenting with what worked best for my child.

No, motherhood is not what I expected to be. It is much harder work, but I can think of no other more meaningful career. After all, our world is directly affected by the people in it and their physical, mental and spiritual well-being. So through their children, mothers have great potential to influence the quality of life in the next generation. What a responsibility! What a joy!

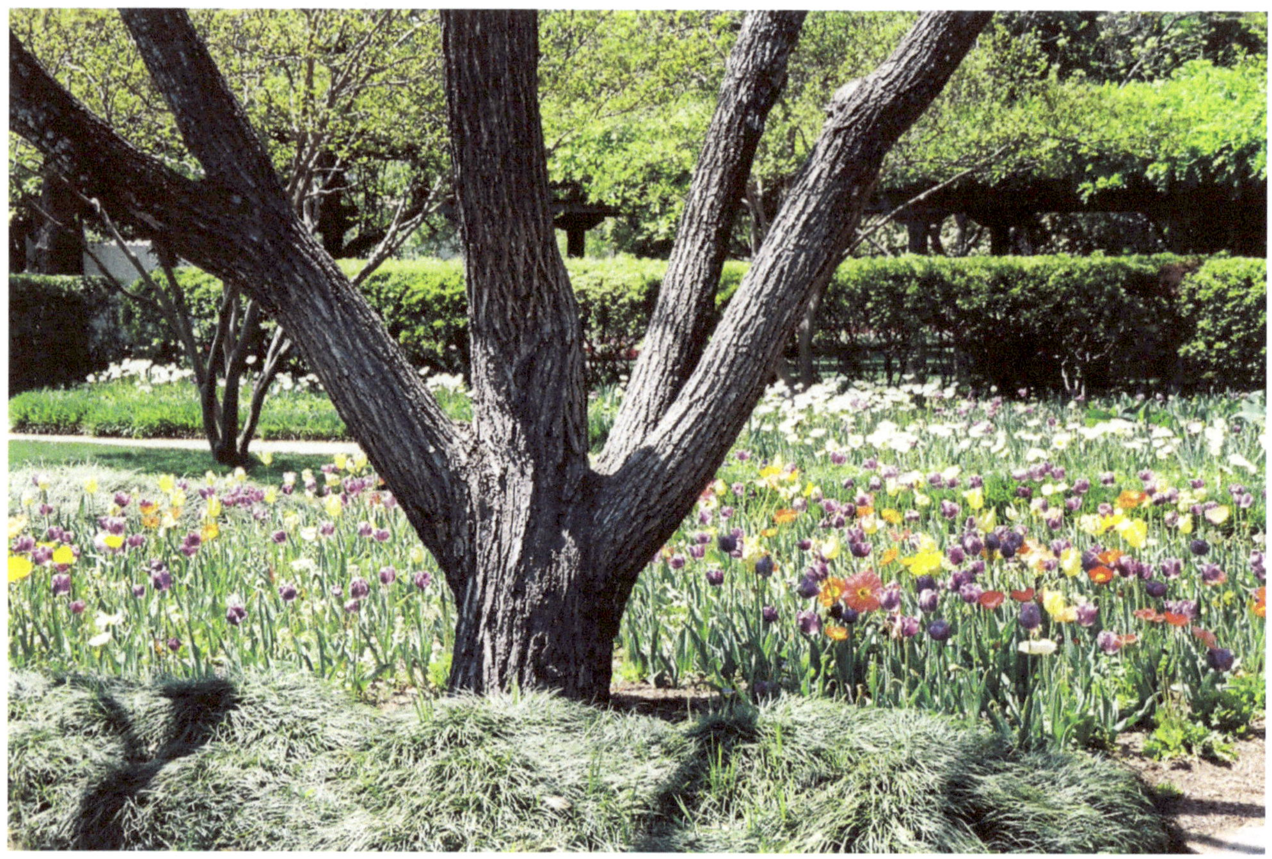

Love is Like a Garden---It Blooms

To love is to encourage whatever makes the other person happy.

To love is to respect the individuality of each other.

To love is to give enough freedom to each other to grow and learn.

To love is to share your feelings in a constructive manner.

To love is to consciously remember all the good in each other.

To love is to accept unconditionally.

Love sets us free to become our best selves.

Just Thinking---A Time to Explore...Love

Do love and marriage go hand-in-hand?

What Love Is:	**What Love is Not:**
Patient	Boastful
Kind	Rude
Unselfish	Easily offended
Courageous	Unforgiving
Hopeful	Glad when others sin
Faithful	Conceited

Marriage customs are not the same in all parts of the world. Not every culture believes that a marriage happens only between people who already love each other. Some cultures have arranged marriages in which the couple may not even be acquainted. But however the marriage begins, the Bible reminds husbands and wives to love each other.

Interestingly enough, love is not just an emotion. As the lists above show, love is an ACTION which does not require a loving feeling to precede it. And that is a good thing, because sometimes we need love even when we don't deserve it. Yes, love and marriage DO go hand-in-hand.

Explore the Bible:

- I Corinthians 13:1-3 explains the importance of love.
- I Corinthians 13:4-7 describes what love looks like.
- I Corinthians 14: 01 teaches that love is the most desired spiritual gift of all.
- Ephesians 5:25-33 instructs a husband to love his wife.
- Titus 2:03 teaches women to be loving wives.

Just Thinking: A Time to Explore...Peace

Quarrels Fits of rage Jealousies Selfish ambitions

Rivalry Spite Hate Cursing

Angry shouting Short-tempered

Bad feelings toward each other

At Christmas time we sing songs that speak of peace and good will on earth. And during the holiday season, we see more good feelings toward our fellow man than any other time of the year. What a shame! Wouldn't it be blissful if we purposely tried to live EVERY day like that? Why don't we?

The Bible has quite a bit to say about all those feelings listed above. In fact, it says that they are a part of our lower nature---and very displeasing to God! Instead of wallowing in these destructive feelings and actions, we are to cultivate things like peace, kindness, and self-control.

Angry shouting...fits of rage...being short-tempered---I do not remember having ever heard a sermon or a lesson about those things. We seldom tend to think about shouting and temper tantrums being displeasing to God. But I can see why they would be distasteful in His mind, because they tend to be so destructive. This must be why the Bible tells us not to let anger lead us into sin.

Explore the Bible:

- Galatians 5:13-25 explains what kinds of things are **not** a part of our best selves. And it lists the desirable attributes that God wants us to nurture.
- Ephesians 4:1-3 tells us to make every effort to live peacefully with others.
- Ephesians 4:31-32 gives instruction to refrain from shouting in anger and every kind of bad feeling toward others. We are to replace these things with tender-heartedness and forgiveness.
- Ephesians 4:26 advises us to resolve our anger quickly, before it has a chance to lead us to do/say something sinful.
- James 1:19-20 instructs us to be a good listener, not getting angry easily.
- James 4:1-5 explains some of the causes of conflicts and quarrels and reminds us that there are better ways to get what we want.

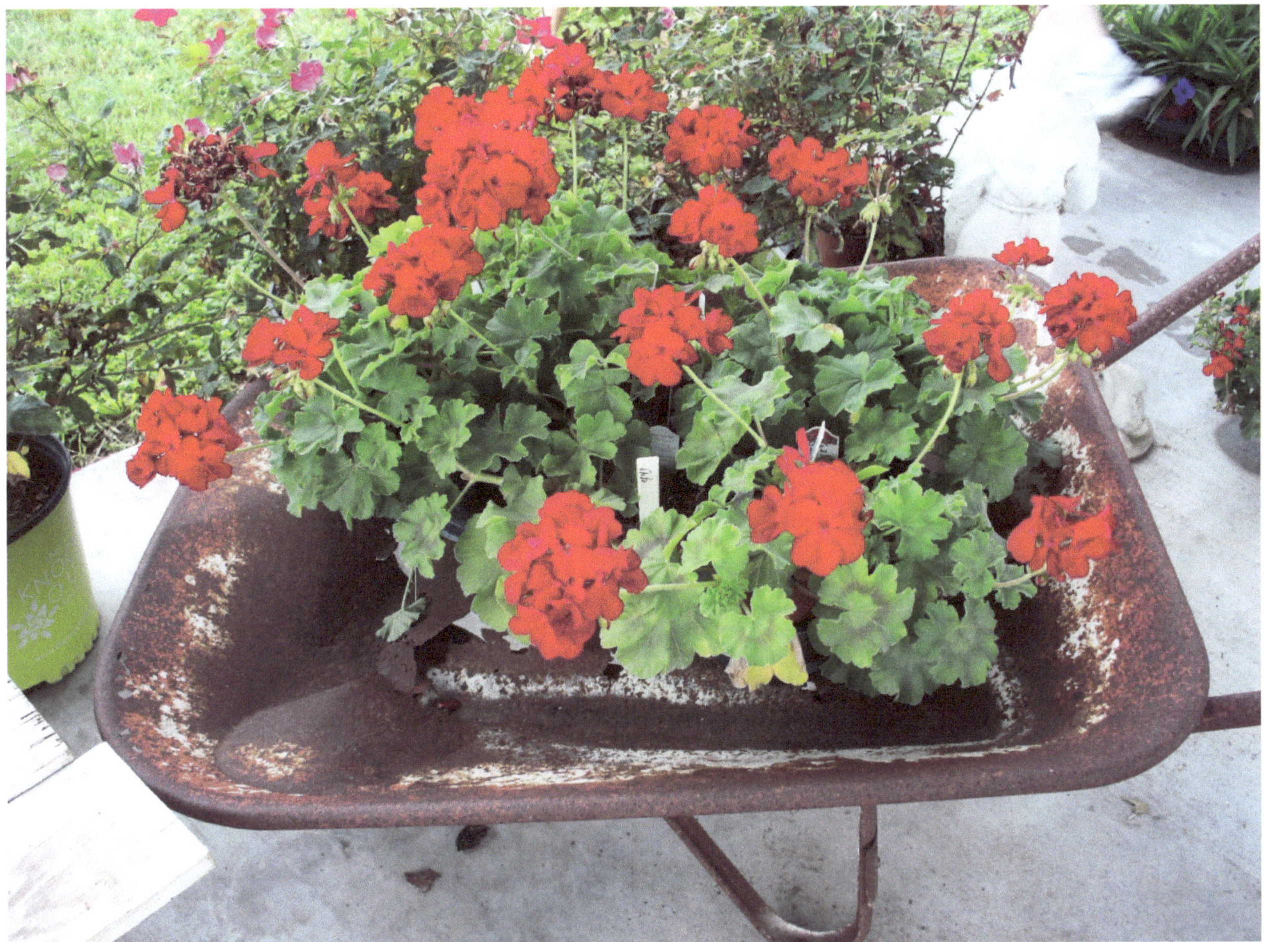

Recipe for a Happy Marriage

GATHER together your ingredients beginning with 1 cup of regard for each other's individuality and 2 cups of sincere praise/compliments. Then **POUR** in generous amounts of the milk of human kindness and 1 gallon of wisdom for building each other up. **SUBSTITUTE** 1 quart of confidence for a pint of panic. **FOLD** in a balance of romance, children and in-laws as well as 1 workable budget, mixed with a generous sprinkling of cooperation. **ADD** 1 cup of contentment, remembering the faults of our mates can spur us to personal growth and don't forget to add 3 teaspoons pure extract of a genuine apology when appropriate.

STIR well, removing unsavory specks of jealousy and criticism. For a sweeter product, add a generous portion of tender caresses and never **SERVE** with a hot tongue or a cold shoulder.

Finally, **COMPLEMENT** the recipe with a heaping bowl of humor!

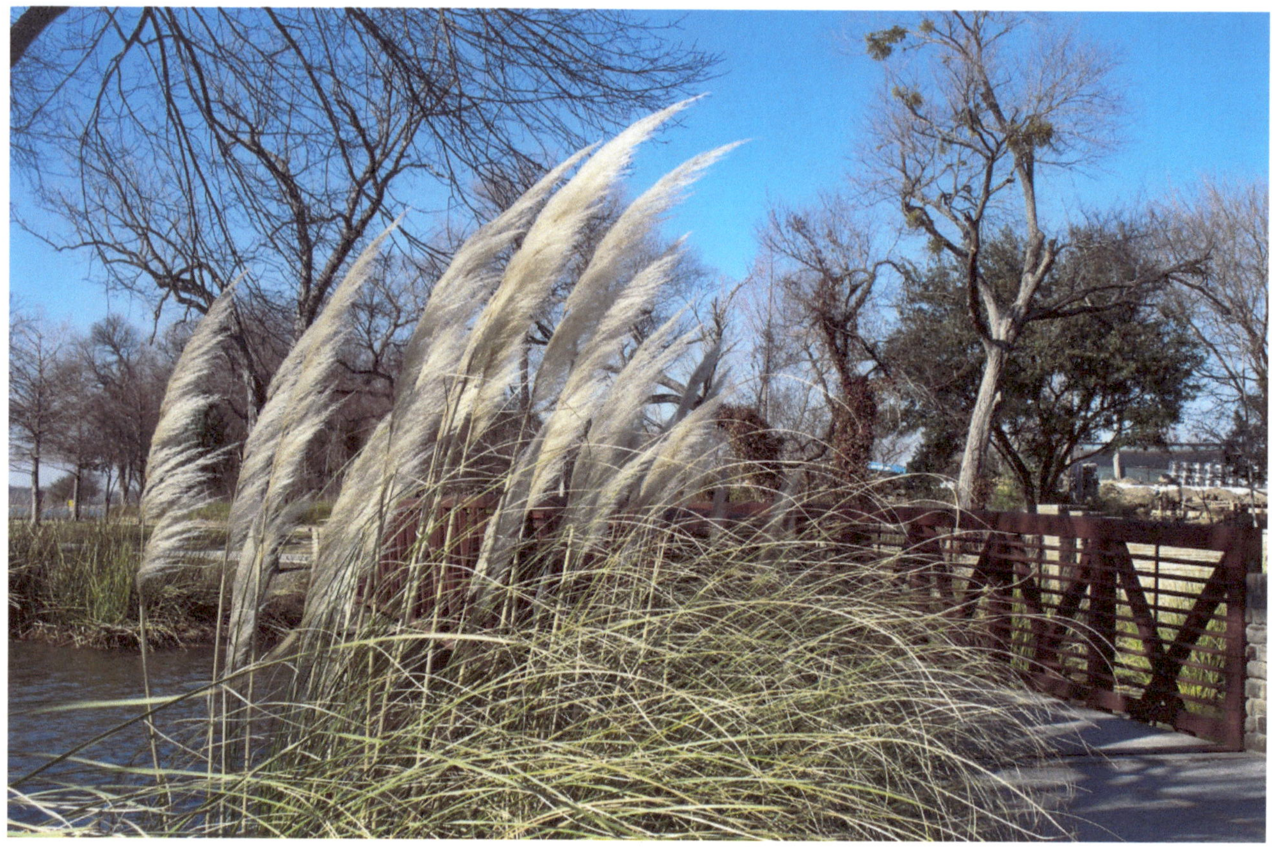

The Great Outdoors

Exercise is a wonderful thing. It strengthens our heart and tones our muscles. It releases stress build-up and decreases depression. It adds quality to our days while it also lengthens our years.

But exercise can become boring. I have tried exercise routines at home, worked out at the gym, and taken swimming lessons. I have included yoga, Pilates, weight training, step aerobics and country western dancing, just to keep from becoming bored. But the thing that works best for me is the great outdoors. That is where I find the most variety.

My favorite place to exercise is at a park---a city park, a state park, or a national park. Pictured above, you can see a photo of the city park where I spend the most time. This is where I hike, bike and kayak. Walking for an hour each day, it takes me about six days to complete the circle around the lake. Every season looks different and every day has its own sites to see---animals, people, sporting events, etc. So it is hard to get bored in a place as vibrant as this. Yes, the park is my own personal work-out gym!

Just Thinking: A Time to Explore…Grace

My spouse just drives me crazy!

Marriage works better when it is sprinkled with heavy doses of grace rather than with resentment. Now, the definition of grace is undeserved favor. And the definition of resentment is irritability. When our spouses irritate us, we have two choices:

- Respond with anger resulting in growing resentment
- Respond with grace resulting in loving forgiveness

Since the Bible instructs us to try to avoid bad feelings of every kind, there must be some ways to do this. Consider these methods to help you apply grace to your marriage:

1. Redefine/expand the attributes that irritate you. For example, if your spouse is stubborn, what are the good things that come out of that general trait? Could it be persistence or tenacity that you appreciate in other venues? If you were to change that trait, how might it alter the good aspects of his/her personality?
2. Look beyond your mate's annoying habits/actions, choosing to see him/her the way God does, with hope for growth in his/her future. Pray for that growth.
3. Celebrate the person that your spouse already is. Then step back, trying not to get in the way of what God is trying to accomplish in her/his life. Be thankful that changing him/her is not YOUR responsibility.
4. Accept you mate's imperfections, without approving of them, remembering that you, also, are not perfect. Forgive your partner even BEFORE she/he engages in the irritating behavior, accepting that this is a part of the person you love.
5. Ask God how He wants YOU to grow from your spouse's imperfections.
6. Reroute your energy by focusing on things that your partner finds irritating about YOU. Consider what you can do about the things that bother your mate. Discuss what each of you can do to be less annoying to each other. Even if one partner is not willing to work together, it may be that his/her attitude will change when you begin to be more sensitive to the way you may be irritating to her/him.
7. Reassess priorities. Ask yourself, "Would this "pet peeve" still be very important to me if I should lose my spouse in death today? "

Explore the Bible:

- Matthew 7: 1-5 reminds us to not to be judgmental of others, remembering that we are also imperfect.
- Matthew 5:07 says it is a blessing to show others mercy, because then, others will show US mercy.

Just Thinking: A Time to Marvel

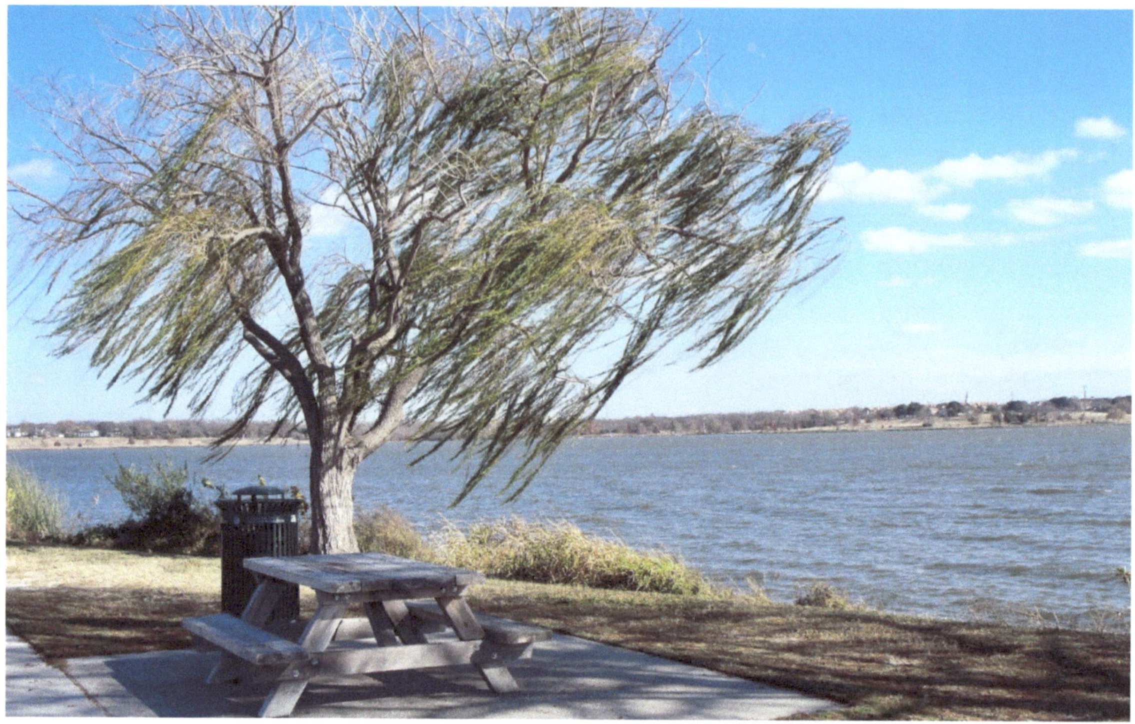

The Gift of Living in the Moment

My father experienced an amazing journey that he shared with his family during their last eight years together. Just prior to that time, personal turmoil had engulfed him for quite a long while. Allow me to show you how God did not forsake him. The story goes like this...It was an ominous day in November when Daddy was transported by helicopter to the hospital for a hemorrhagic stroke. Somehow, he survived, but the next few months would prove to be a fight for his life. Finally, over a year later he was released to go home. During the following full year, he would continue several types of therapy at home on a regular basis to help him walk again, etc. He remained unable to speak and had problems with short-term memory, but by his 50th wedding anniversary he was able to dance with my mother at the large party given by my siblings and myself. On that day, the smile on his face and the lilt in his step revealed his joy better than any words he could have spoken! Of course, there were both set-backs and joys during those last eight years. But, all in all, he remained strong and physically active-still able to enjoy his life. And he DID enjoy each day! In fact, the short-term memory issue was a blessing in disguise. The turmoil in his life no longer was a problem, because he could only focus on the present. If something upset him, he did not remember it for long. He was finally free to enjoy each moment as it presented itself. Apparently, God used Daddy's health to bring back his peace of mind! I call that "amazing grace"!

Just Thinking: A Time to Explore...Careers

Is God interested in my occupation?

As a boss, what does God expect of me?

The Bible actually does have some things to say about our work lives as listed below:

- We are expected to earn the respect of others by not being lazy.
- We are to work at jobs that are honorable.
- We are to be honest in our occupations.
- We are to treat subordinates with respect.
- We are to work conscientiously for our employers.
- We are to respect a boss's position, even when we cannot respect his actions.

Clearly, our careers are important to God, because the Bible discusses it in detail. It is part of God's design that management must take responsibility for the everyday tasks that will bring income to a company and its employees. Along with extra responsibilities, He has also given employers/bosses certain restrictions and guidelines. Furthermore, God expects employees to cultivate a good attitude, as well as to produce the work they are being paid to accomplish. The Bible reminds us that even when circumstances are not ideal, we can find honor and joy in our work, if we do it in a way that serves others and with an attitude that brings honor to God.

Explore the Bible:

- 1 Thessalonians 4:11-12 directs us to work in order to earn the respect of others.
- Titus 3:08 says that we are to choose honorable occupations.
- Titus 3:14 reminds us to find honest employment to earn money for our necessities.
- Ephesians 6:09 tells employers/bosses to treat subordinates well, not harshly, remembering that God is over both the staff AND the executives.
- Colossians 3:25 instructs bosses to be both just and fair with their employees.
- Colossians 3:22-24 says that employees are to put their whole heart into their work.
- I Peter 2:17-18 instructs employees to accept the authority of their bosses, even when the bosses are hard to live with.
- Ephesians 6:5-8 directs employees to give cheerful service to their bosses, knowing that God will bless the employee for good work.

Just Thinking: A Time to Explore...Trials

Does God care about my troubles?

Why Does He Allow Suffering?

How can I survive the pain?

Probably the most significant thing I have discovered as an adult is how God can use pain, hardships, and grief to make something beautiful. Problems can be the doorway to the future---a richer one than we could even imagine. Life is not the same after a tragedy, but it can be very good again.

God is never responsible for the bad things that happen in our lives; there are many reasons why we sometimes suffer. But He knows how to turn those things around so that they can be used for our ultimate good. I have learned to joyfully anticipate the outcomes of the trials in my own life, because watching how God intervenes is much like living right in the middle of an awesome adventure! When I purposely think of pain and hardships and grief in that way, it is a form of trusting God. And trust is something very dear to our Creator's heart!

Explore the Bible:

- Romans 8:35-39 tells us there is nothing bad enough that can separate us from the loving care of God, our Heavenly Father.
- James 5:11 says that the Lord (God) is full of compassion.
- Corinthians 10:13 promises that God will not allow us to face anything that we are not equipped to handle.
- Romans 8:28 assures us that God can use hardships to ultimately benefit us.
- 1 Peter 1:6-7 explains that trials of all kinds are useful to help our faith to grow.
- Ephesians 6:10-18 reminds us to find our strength in God's unlimited power and to pray about all our concerns.
- 2 Peter 2:07 notes that God is easily able to rescue us when we are in trouble.
- Phillipians 4:13 tells us that we have the strength to triumph over anything through God's power.
- James 5:13 instructs all those who are in trouble to pray for assistance.
- 1 Peter 5:6-11 reassures us that our suffering will not last indefinitely.

Just Thinking: A Time to Marvel

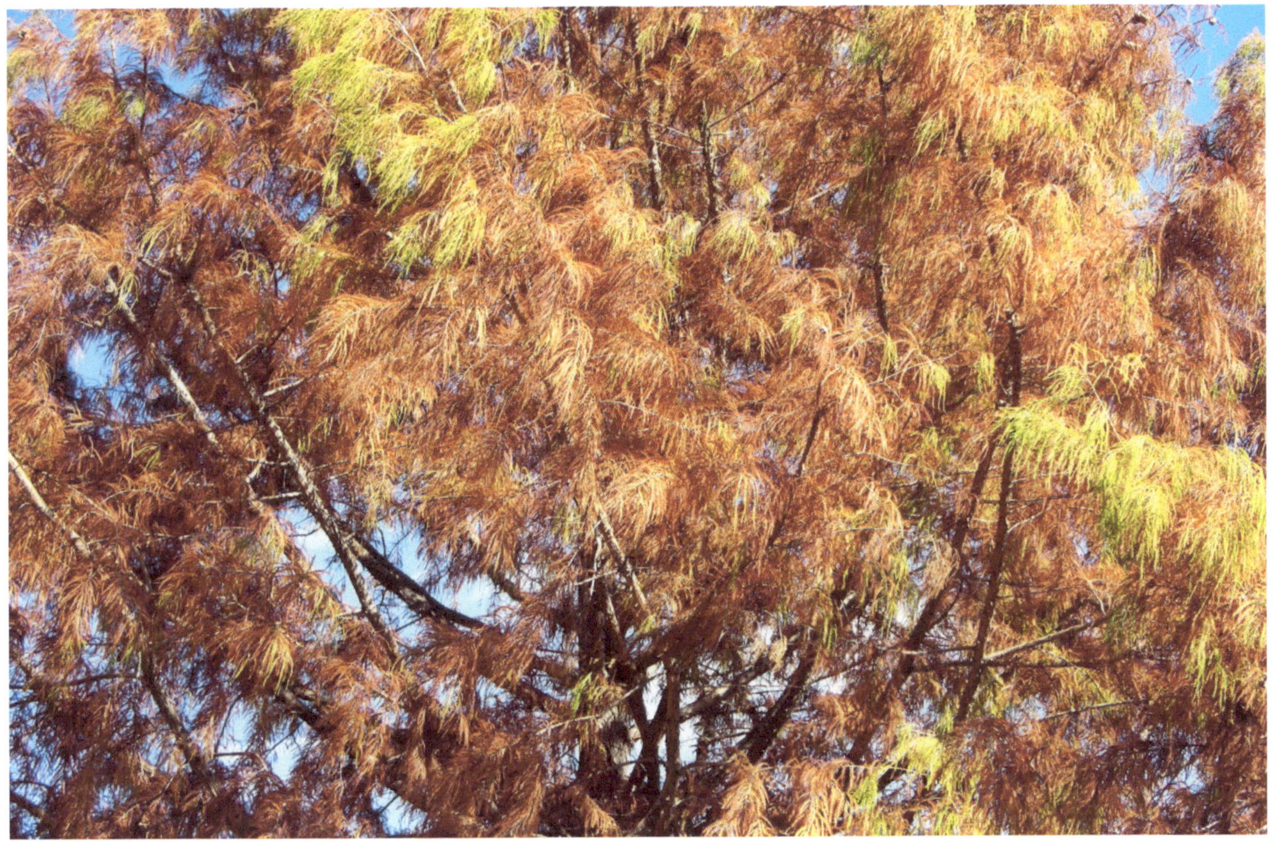

Finding Gold in the Process

Sometimes it is not possible to build something new and better while the old structure is still in place. There was a time when it became necessary for me to leave behind what was toxic in my life and to rebuild it. It was not something that could be accomplished quickly, because it often takes time to heal from wounds or tragedies. So it helps to relax and try to enjoy the process.

These are the methods that helped me to do that more effectively:

- Blocking out time segments for accomplishments
- Living in the moment, rather than in the past
- Practicing a positive attitude
- Trusting that God's purpose is being worked out

Keeping a calendar diary during that time, I eventually realized that every entry helped to weave a tale that became clear as time went on---a tale that revealed a heavenly plan that God already had in store!

Just Thinking: A Time to Explore...Faith 22-a

What is faith?

Is God offended when I struggle without Him?

How much faith do I need?

Is God really capable of the impossible?

Faith means believing something that you cannot see. It means trusting in something/someone. Like any loving parent, God desires to be trusted, because He is trustworthy. So, without faith, it is not possible to please Him. The Bible tells us that we only need a little faith to accomplish the unthinkable. And we are assured that God can do far more than we could possibly imagine.

It seems like having faith would be difficult, but I have learned that it is actually less stressful to exercise faith than to live in fear or uncertainty. Why would I want to choose the harder way to live?

Choosing to exercise faith is like exercising my body---it gets stronger and stronger with practice. Every time God answers one of my prayers, it builds my faith for the next time. And it gets easier to come to Him for my needs/desires. So, if I want more faith, I can get it by:

- asking God to increase my faith
- stepping out in faith
- watching how God answers my prayers

Explore the Bible:

- Hebrews 11:01 explains that faith is the evidence of things that we hope for but cannot see with our eyes.
- Hebrews 11:06 tells us that, without faith, we cannot please God.
- Matthew 17:20 assures us that it takes only a tiny amount of faith to be effective.
- Ephesians 3:20 speaks of God's immeasurable ability to answer our prayer requests.

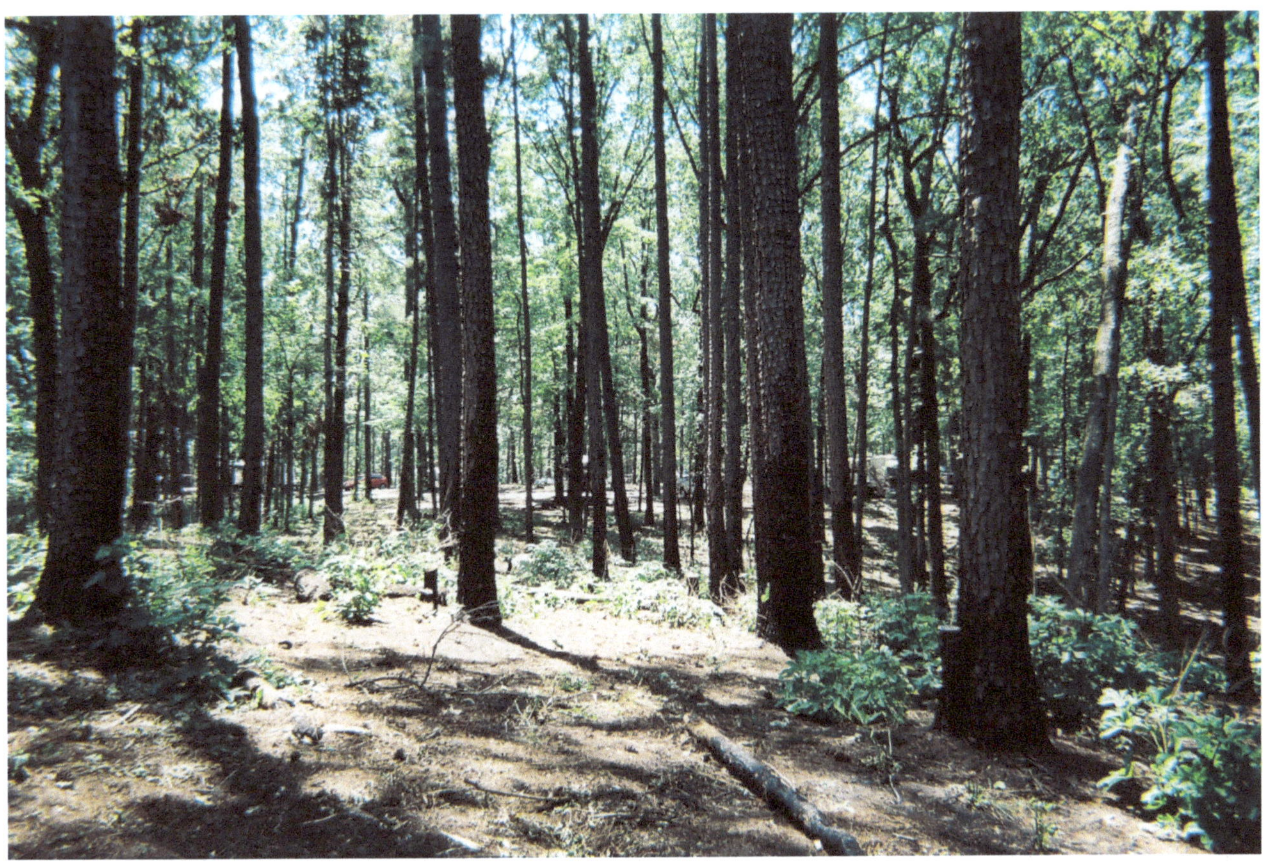

Chasing Dreams

When the decision was made to move out of state, my family of origin spent the first two years living in the city. But my dad hankered to return to his first love--- farming. So we began a life on a farm that would include 3 hens and a rooster, 3 pigs, a Jersey milk cow, a Hereford calf with his mother and a vegetable garden. We learned to make many adjustments. For example, my sisters and I routinely helped to hand-pump our water for daily consumption, because there was no running water in our four-room house. Mother washed the baby's diapers in an old-fashioned wringer washer on the back porch and hung them out on the backyard clothes line to dry. But the outdoor toilet was probably the biggest adjustment of all. Now we were a modern family who was willing to turn back the clock to a more primitive style of living--all for the sake of a dream! During the last year that we spent in the country setting, my siblings and I worked in our dad's soybean fields, helping him save enough money for our family to move back to town! I am sure Daddy was disappointed, but his short-lived dream did produce some unexpected rewards; it taught his children the wisdom of frugality, the art of appreciation for what we have, and the benefits of family teamwork! Those things would make a rich legacy to leave to ANY child!

Just Thinking: A Time to Explore...Worry

Is God really interested in my problems?

Is there a remedy for worry?

According to Merriam-Webster's Pocket Dictionary, the words listed below all mean the same thing; but whichever word is used, it is all about FEAR.

- Concern (mild intensity)
- Worry (moderate intensity)
- Anxiety (severe intensity)

There are differences in the intensity of fear. We can be concerned about something without being worried or feeling anxious. In my mind, to be concerned means to realize there is something that must be addressed. To be worried means that the concern has escalated to something to be fearful about. And to be anxious, means that fear has increased to the point of a feeling of apprehension that pervades a large part of our thoughts.

The Bible has much to say about fear. In fact, it speaks of a number of different kinds of worry:

- Legitimate concerns about our physical needs
- Frivolous concerns about having the trendiest cars/clothes/electronics, etc.
- Excessive concerns about the future, rather than living in the moment

Explore the Bible:

- Matthew 6:25-33 tells us not to worry about our needs being met.
- I Peter 5:6-7 reminds us that we should go to God in prayer when we have a concern, because He is in charge of our welfare.
- Philippians 4:6-7 explains that we can have relief from anxiety if we will pray to God about those things that frighten us, reminding us to be sure to thank God for answered prayer.
- Hebrews 13:5-6 instructs us not to make the pursuit of material possessions to be a priority, but to be content with what we have.
- Matthew 6:34 encourages us to live in the moment, one day at a time, knowing that each day already contains enough problems of its own.

Just Thinking: A Time to Marvel

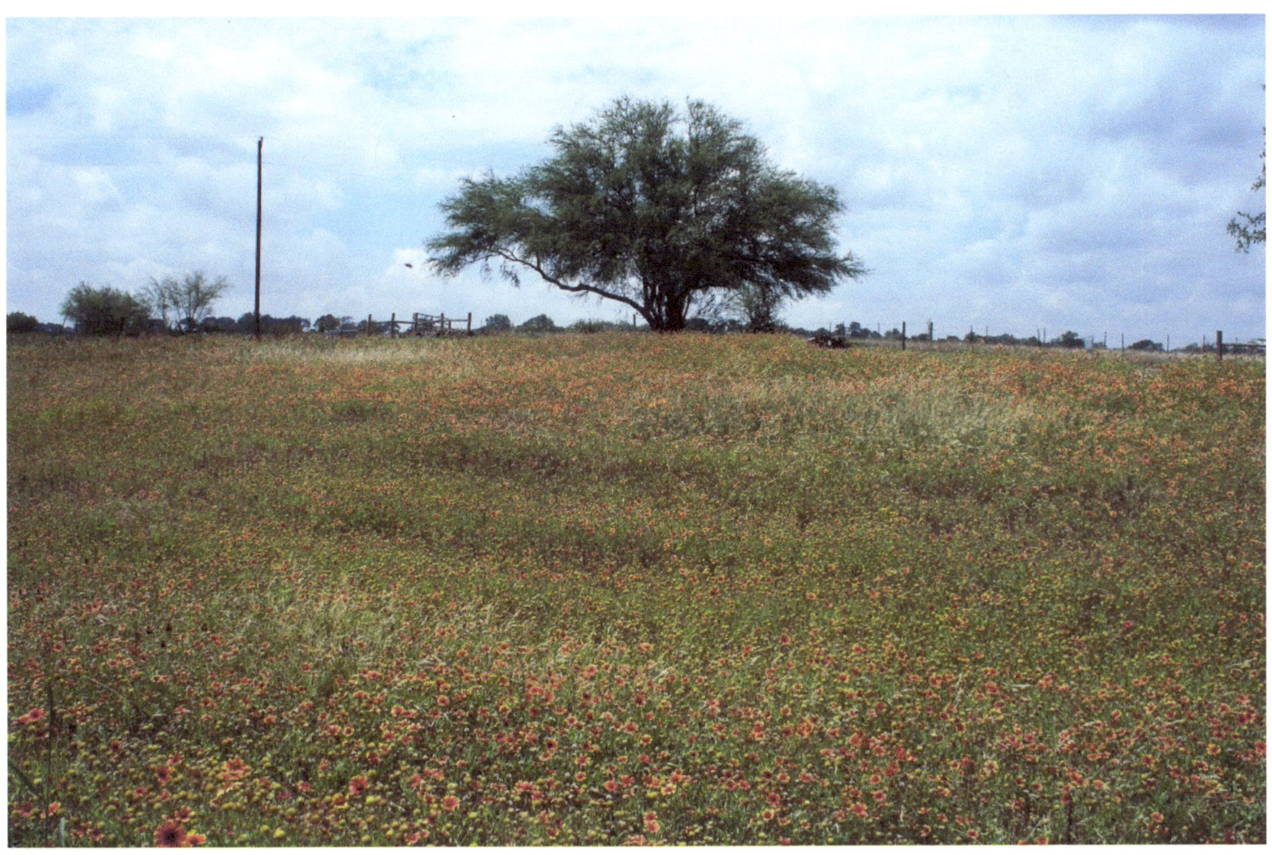

The Flowers of the Field

I like to keep abreast of modern medical science. One of the things that I have learned is that medication is not the prescription of choice for anxiety. Behavior modification, like the steps listed here, are the first line of treatment when anxiety is out of control.

Prescription for Worry:

- Aerobic exercise---Practice this activity for at least 30 minutes daily. It helps to reduce the build-up of tension that is so uncomfortable and so unhealthy.
- Compartmentalization---Choose to spend time thinking about the solution or answer for a limited amount of time. View it as an adventure, asking God to give you wisdom and discernment.
- Distraction---Once you have compartmentalized the issue, then just focus on the moment, concentrating on the tasks at hand. Consider it as an exercise in faith.

Remember---If God is aware of the needs of even the flowers in the field, then how much more important are the needs of His loved ones?

Notes

Photography:

The author has chosen to use her personal amateur photography efforts, shown in this book, to create an atmosphere of quiet reflection which can enhance her readers' spiritual journey.

Notes

Photography:

Just Thinking: Book Dedication Prayer

Dear God,

CONTENT: May Your name be honored in this book. Please let Your will be done through all the thoughts expressed in it. Guide me in what I write from cover to cover, because I realize that you hold me responsible for how I reflect You to others. I pray that I will be successful in following all of Your directions.

PROCESS: A wise person once gave me instruction on how to build something new. A referral was made to the instructions You gave to Noah on how to build the ark in preparation for the world-wide flood that was to come. The plans were laid out far in advance and every detail was covered. It is obvious that a project will not end well if it was not started right. At the very least, it is likely to be fraught with mishap and delays. But the way to start right is to consult You for the plan from the beginning. That is what I am doing today, God. I pray that I will know and follow Your plan for this book from start to finish.

SAFTEY: I believe that You have the necessary knowledge, wisdom and insight that I lack. Starting with the content of this book, to its publication and finally to its distribution, etc., I ask You to please keep me, as the author, safe from any dangers or serious snags along the way.

OTHER NEEDS: Because I do not know exactly what to request or how to pray, I also ask for whatever else You know I need from now on, regarding this book project.

THANKSGIVING: Thank you, God, for listening to this prayer. And I thank you, in advance, for answering it. In Jesus' name I pray, knowing that He made it possible for me to speak directly to You today. Amen.

By Cathy Foster Brown

Seek Ask Receive

www.ingramcontent.com/pod-product-compliance
Lightning Source LLC
LaVergne TN
LVHW070151110826
845147LV00002B/373
9780578137230